A Pictorial Tribute to the

NATIONAL BUS COMPANY 1981

Three dual-purpose Seddon RU Pennine bodied vehicles of the Crosville fleet, stand in the Northwich Crosville garage on 29th August 1981. All three vehicles carry the 'Mid-Cheshire' local identity name introduced on 10th February 1980 at Northwich garage. The Seddons on view inside the garage are Nos. EPG729 (OFM 729K), EPG727 (OFM 727K), and EPG728 (OFM 728K). The 'Mid-Cheshire' name was derived from the Mid-Cheshire Motor Bus Company taken over by the North Western Road Car Company in 1923, Northwich of course originally being a North Western garage. A Leyland National of the Crosville fleet has now been painted in the original livery of this company, blue with a cream skirt, and is allocated to Northwich garage.

Rex Kennedy

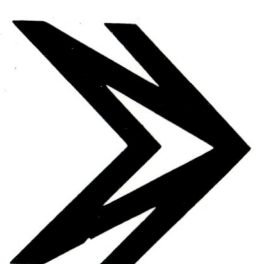

A Pictorial Tribute to the
NATIONAL BUS COMPANY
1981

D.R. Kennedy
and
A. Kennedy

◁ Frontispiece:
An East Kent 13 ft. 8 in. Bristol VRT, No. 7658 (XJJ 658V), fitted with ECW bodywork, passes through the narrow West Gate at Canterbury on 23rd November 1981. The West Gate was completed in 1380 and is situated at the river crossing. It incorporates some Roman brickwork and for 400 years until 1829 was used as the city gaol. In recent years it has been a museum with a collection of arms, cycles and implements of torture on view.

Rex Kennedy

Above:
A 1967 Bristol RELL6G, No. 3239 (PYG 657E), of the West Yorkshire fleet, passes beneath the city walls of York at Easter in 1981. This vehicle, which has been withdrawn since the picture was taken, carries the now no longer used York-West Yorkshire fleetname and is also fitted with the flat windscreen of the earlier Bristol RE models.

Andrew Kennedy

All rights reserved. No part of this publication may be reproduced, stored in retrieval system or transmitted, in any form or by any means, electronic, mechanical, photocopying, recording or otherwise, without the prior permission of Oxford Publishing Company.

© Oxford Publishing Company and
D. R. & A. J. Kennedy 1982

ISBN 86093 170 6

CONTENTS

	Plate Nos.
Alder Valley	1–9
Bristol	10–21
Crosville	22–35
Cumberland	36–40
Eastern Counties	41–50
Eastern National	51–58
East Kent	59–70
East Midland/Mansfield	71–78
East Yorkshire	79–85
Hants & Dorset/Provincial/Shamrock & Rambler	86–102
Lincolnshire	103–107
London Country/Greenline	108–123
Maidstone & District	124–131
Midland Red	132–145
National Welsh (Cymru Cenedlaethol) Jones of Aberbeeg	146–163
Northern	164–172
Oxford/South Midland	173–185
Potteries (PMT)	186–196
Ribble	197–205
Southdown	206–213
Southern Vectis/Fountain Coaches	214–220
South Wales (De Cymru)	221–229
Trent	230–240
United	241–250
United Counties	251–265
Western National/Devon General/Royal Blue Greenslades	266–282
West Riding/Yorkshire	283–293
West Yorkshire	294–306
Yorkshire Traction	307–313
National Travel (East)	314–316
National Travel (London)	317–318
National Travel (South West)/Wessex	319–323
National Travel (West)	324–326

Printed by:
B. H. Blackwell Limited
in the City of Oxford

Published by:
Oxford Publishing Co.,
Link House,
West Street,
Poole,
Dorset.

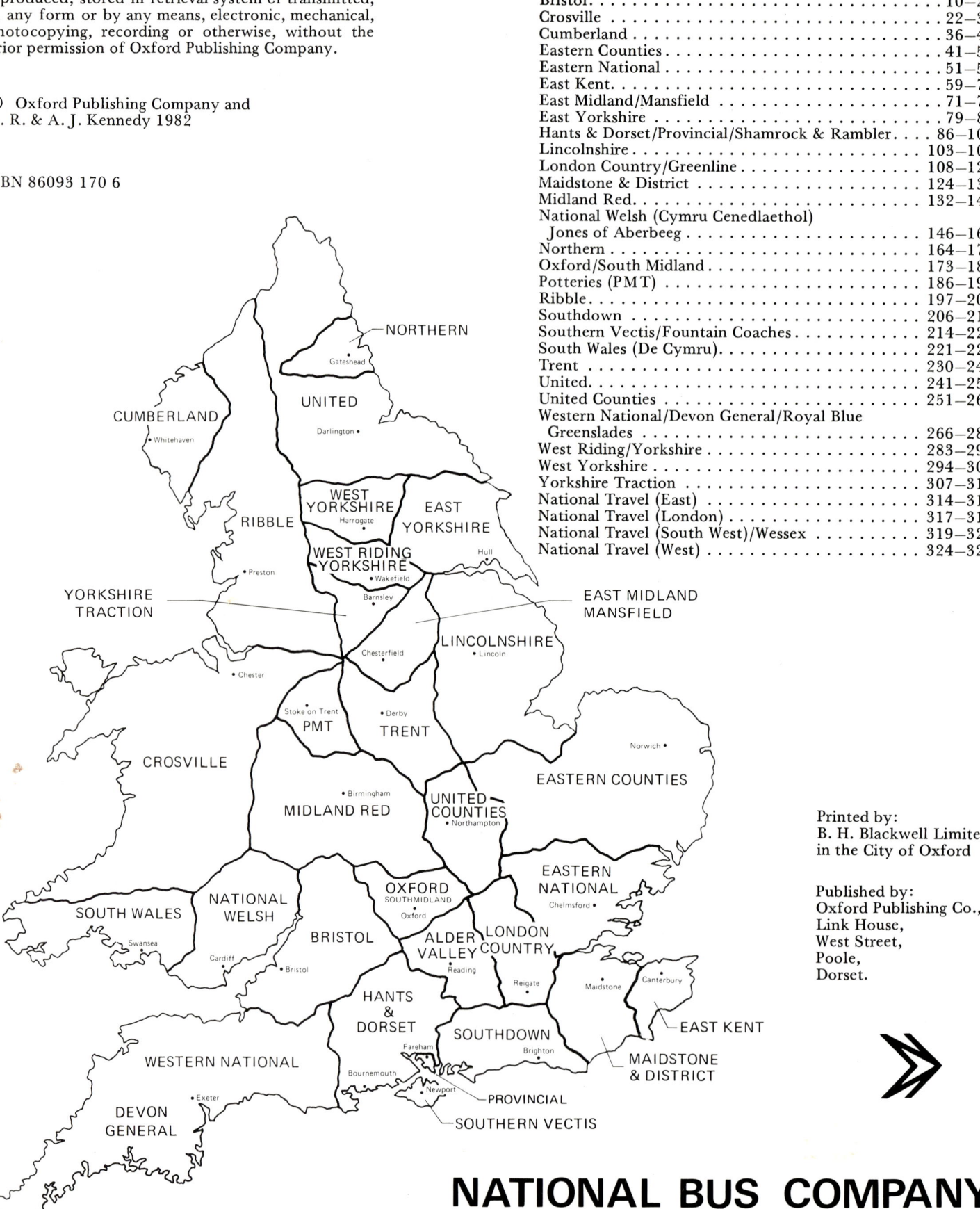

NATIONAL BUS COMPANY
operating networks indicating main headquarters
(excluding National Travel)

INTRODUCTION

The National Bus Company, during 1981, provided interesting changes within its vast network with the introduction of the Leyland 'Olympian' double decker and the building of the last Bristol VR which, it is hoped, the 'Olympian' will replace. The Bristol FLF, much loved amongst enthusiasts, is fast disappearing, with the only NBC fleets now using these vehicles in any quantity being Bristol Omnibus Co. and Eastern Counties. We have moved into 1982 without the sight of the AEC Regent Vs of East Kent and South Wales on service and even the Bristol LH is gradually reducing in numbers every month. The older design double deckers now seem to end their days as trainee vehicles or open toppers at seaside holiday resorts. In this album, every photograph has been taken in 1981 throughout the various seasons of the year and we have tried to portray many of the changes, both in vehicle design and livery, which occurred during 1981. My 16 year old son, Andrew, and I, have endeavoured to put together a collection of photographs portraying buses and coaches from every subsidiary in the NBC network, coupled with detailed captions containing information we have acquired on the vehicles and companies included. During 1981, Andrew and I travelled many miles throughout Britain and visited over 200 locations. We saw more vehicles appear in original fleet liveries commemorating anniversaries of now NBC companies, and saw vehicles change hands within the NBC fleet and arrive from other operators in Britain. We have photographed in rain, snow and sunshine and, in the photographic content of this album, have portrayed vehicles on service, both in town and country, vehicles at bus stations, on garages, under maintenance and with driver training in progress. Whilst preparing the captions, Andrew and I have unearthed a great deal of information in addition to our own previous knowledge by reference to authorities and to particular NBC companies and their employees. Andrew and I have spent hours of pleasure travelling the roads of Britain from the Yorkshire Dales to the West Country and from the Welsh Valleys to East Anglia incorporating many interesting town visits. Our thanks go to the few enthusiasts who have assisted us by providing photographs of particular vehicles and locations to make this book complete. The father and son team of myself and Andrew has been a pleasurable experience, not only in travelling around together and seeing the NBC changes as they occurred, but also in researching and compiling an album of this nature. Our thanks also go to the PSV Circle who regularly provide their members with updated information which is invaluable and are an organisation we can truly recommend to any bus enthusiast. Finally, we should like to dedicate this book to my wife, Pauline, who once said 'Why don't you take more photographs of buses?' The result is this book, which, without Andrew's invaluable research, would not have been so informative. Our photographic exploits have resulted in Pauline either spending many a Saturday and Sunday alone or sitting in the car awaiting our return from a photographic session.

Rex Kennedy
Oxford
1982

A variety of National Welsh designs line up in Tredegar garage on 23rd July 1981. On view are three Bristol VRs, two Leyland Nationals, a Plaxton bodied coach and two styles of Bristol RE, an RELH and an RESL. The vehicles age from 1967 to 1980. Tredegar garage follows the trend of certain other National Welsh garages such as Monmouth, Abergavenny, Bridgend and Cinderford in having the bus station adjacent to the garage buildings.

Rex Kennedy

ALDER VALLEY

Plate 1: An Alder Valley dual-doored Bristol RESL 40 seater, No. 467 (CHO 699K), stands parked alongside a 1974 Leyland National 11.3 metre Mk. 1, No. 181 (GPC 730N), at Newbury bus station on 19th November 1981. No. 467 was built in 1971 and is an ex-Aldershot & District vehicle. The fleetname 'Kennetbus', carried by both vehicles in this picture, denotes allocation to Newbury garage and was introduced on 17th February 1980. The majority of fleetnames now carried within NBC companies, are as the result of the Market Analysis Projects introduced in the mid-1970s. The Midland Red Fleet initially pioneered the use of these local identity names. The Alder Valley vehicles carry their fleetnames on fablon stickers, whereas some other companies have these names painted directly on to the bus.

Rex Kennedy

Plate 2: Two Alder Valley buses were painted, at the end of 1980, in the original Aldershot & District livery to commemorate 75 years of service. The livery was two-tone green with the original style of fleetname. In addition to No. 611 (GGM 81W), a Bristol VRT pictured at Reading bus station on 30th January 1981, a 1975 Leyland National Mk. 1, No. 231 (KPA 382P), was also painted in a similar livery. No. 611 is of the lowbridge variety and is allocated to Aldershot garage. Aldershot & District took over the assets of Thames Valley Traction Co. Ltd. on 1st January 1972 after both companies had been incorporated into the NBC fleet in January 1969. The new fleetname 'Alder Valley' was introduced and the headquarters moved to Reading.

Andrew Kennedy

Thames line

Plate 3: A snowbound Alder Valley 1975 Leyland National stands dejected in the yard at Maidenhead garage on 13th December 1981 during the very cold spell of weather which this area faced before Christmas. The blind displaying 'Not In Service' on locally allocated No. 199 (HPK 501N) says it all!
Rex Kennedy

Plate 4: Soon after crossing the River Thames at Maidenhead, on Sunday 13th December 1981, an Alder Valley 11.3 metre Leyland National Mk. 1, No. 121 (KCG 621L), continues its journey to Slough. The snow-clad houses and trees create a Christmas-like setting.
Rex Kennedy

Plate 7: Former North Western Road Car Co. 1971 Leyland Leopard with Alexander 'Y' type body, No. 366 (SJA 366J), stands at Victoria coach station in January 1981. Five of these vehicles were transferred to Alder Valley in 1980 to help out on Londonlink services pending deliveries of new vehicles. The vehicle carries the smart dual-purpose livery with the red band and is classified as a coach. It is noticeable that she still carries the old North Western fleet number at this stage, and was renumbered in May 1981 to 56. Before being acquired by Alder Valley, No. 366 was delivered new to the North Western Road Car Co., passed to National Travel (North Western) in 1974 and to National Travel (West) in April 1979.

Kevin Lane

◁ **Plate 5:** Newbury town centre complete with its Christmas decorations, as Alder Valley 'Kennetbus', No. 176 (TBL 176M), a 1974 Leyland National wends its way down the main street. Other local fleetnames used by Alder Valley are; Aldershot & District (Aldershot garage), Wessexway (Alton), Forestride (Bracknell), Weyfarer (Guildford and Woking), Chilternlink (High Wycombe), Downsman (Hindhead) and Thamesline (Maidenhead).

Rex Kennedy

◁ **Plate 6:** An Alton based Alder Valley 1980 Bristol VRT, No. 627 (GGM 107W), bearing the 'Wessexway' fleetname, awaits departure for Southampton in Farnham town centre in December 1981. The Amery Street garage at Alton, used today, was one of the Aldershot & District depots before the amalgamation with Thames Valley.

Ian Pringle

Plate 8: Certain Alder Valley Bristol VRT double deckers carry the predominant white livery seen in this view of No. 981 (CJH 121V), at Reading bus station on 30th January 1981. This is an attractive variation of the NBC dual-purpose livery and coach seating is fitted. Alongside No. 981 is another Alder Valley Bristol VRT, No. 960 (WJM 820T), bearing the standard red livery and the Forestride fleetname.

Andrew Kennedy

Plate 9: Two members of the Alder Valley coach fleet rest in the parking area at Aldershot garage on 18th October 1981. The more modern coach, No. 94 (WJM 814T), sports the attractive yellow, red, blue and white livery used on the Railair Link services, but does not carry 'Railair Link' on the front or sides. The vehicle is a 1979 Leyland Leopard PSU3 with Plaxton bodywork. Parked alongside is ex-Thames Valley Bristol RELH, No. 64 (CJB 590J), with Plaxton body, built in 1971 and painted in the standard white coach livery.

Rex Kennedy

BRISTOL

Plate 10: At the busy Swindon bus station, a locally allocated Bristol RE, No. SN 1084 (OHW 596F), of the Bristol Omnibus fleet, prepares to move off empty on 13th August 1981. This particular vehicle is fitted with the flat windscreen whereas the Bristol RE in the distance has the curved screen in addition to carrying different route indicator panels. Both vehicles have ECW bodywork.
Rex Kennedy

Plate 11: The first of five MCW Metrobuses purchased by Bristol Omnibus Company resplendent in the 'Farecard Advertising' livery, stands adjacent to Bath bus station on 2nd July 1981. All five of these vehicles are allocated to Bath garage and are powered by Rolls Royce engines. No. 6000 (DAE 510W), after delivery to Bath, commenced driver familiarisation on the first day of January 1981, entering service 10 days later. It sports a yellow front with black edging to a white 'V'. The rear of the bus is dark red. The other MCW vehicles in this series carry varying rear end colours: No. 6001 (dark blue), 6002 (green), 6003 (orange) and 6004 (yellow).
Andrew Kennedy

Plate 12: Ex-Oxford/South Midland 1968 Daimler Fleetline, with Northern Counties bodywork, now in the Bristol fleet, No. WM 7001 (KFC 373G), passes along the sea front at Weston-super-Mare on a cold 20th October 1981. This vehicle was one of three of the same design bought in 1981 from Oxford/South Midland by Bristol Omnibus Co. all of which were allocated to Weston-super-Mare. Whilst in the City of Oxford fleet this vehicle was numbered 373 and was one of the first batch of rear engined double deckers bought by this company. The unusual moulding beneath the upper and lower windows shows the area within which the City of Oxford duck-egg green colour bands were located. This sea front is, of course, crowded with holidaymakers and cars during the height of the summer and the bus station and garage lie on the opposite carriageway.

Rex Kennedy

Plate 13: One of the major strongholds of NBC Bristol FLF Lodekkas is the City of Bristol. These vehicles can still be seen in abundance on the Filton and Patchway routes to and from the city centre, and out past Lawrence Hill garage towards Kingswood. Allocations during late 1981 are at the Bristol Omnibus garages at Muller Road, Winterstoke Road and Lawrence Hill. The FLFs first entered production in 1959, and the letters indicate; F (flat floor), L (long wheelbase) and F (front entrance). This view shows Muller Road based No. 7241 (FHT 16D) in Colston Avenue, Bristol preparing to leave with a Filton service on 29th September 1981. No. MR 7241 is a 1966 model which was actually withdrawn from service on 31st October 1980 and reinstated in January 1981. All FLFs are driver and conductor operated as one man operation cannot be instigated owing to the half-cab design.

Graham Wise

Plate 14: The recovery vehicle seen alongside the Bristol Omnibus Co. garage at Stroud on 24th August 1981 is No. W144, (ex-2114), a 1961 Bristol MW6G originally fitted with a 39 seat ECW coach body. It was converted to a recovery vehicle in May 1973 and was one of a batch of five, three of which, Nos. 2111, 2113 and 2114, were converted in this manner. It is pleasing to see this design of vehicle still in existence even if only in this form.

Rex Kennedy

Plate 17: Prior to departure for Swindon, 1970 Bristol RE, No. SN 516 (YHT 802J), stands in the market square in Faringdon, Oxfordshire on a sunny 31st October 1981. This service, operated by the Bristol Omnibus Co., is a connecting service with the Oxford/South Midland service from Witney to Faringdon, thereby enabling passengers to travel conveniently between Witney and Swindon. In addition, there is a Bristol Omnibus Co. service between Swindon and Oxford.

Andrew Kennedy

Plate 15: Parked at the rear of Stroud garage on 24th August 1981 is the only Leyland Redline 440EA in the Bristol fleet carrying a 17 seat Ascough body. Now bearing the fleet number 301, with the 'G' obliterated, this vehicle, Regn. No. PHU 647M, once bore the fleet number G402 when used in late 1973 on the Mini Centrebus Service in Gloucester. In this view No. 301 carries the Windmill Hill, Totterdown Community Bus symbol and was obviously used on this service in the Bristol area prior to being moved to Stroud. The 'G' prefix to fleet numbers indicates allocation to the Gloucester 'City' fleet.

Rex Kennedy

Plate 16: Standing outside Bath railway station on 2nd July 1981 is a Bath based Bristol Omnibus Company 1977 Leyland PSU3 with Plaxton bodywork, No. 2311 (PWS 492S). This vehicle carries the dual-purpose green and white livery and was originally numbered 2188.

Andrew Kennedy

Plate 18: On 28th November 1981, a Bristol Omnibus Co. 1973 Leyland National, No. CM 3083 (JHU 873L) passes through Cheltenham town centre. This vehicle was converted from a dual-doored version to the front entrance single door type and on conversion was renumbered from 1432. The festive spirit is apparent as children enjoy the amusements on the pavement.

Rex Kennedy

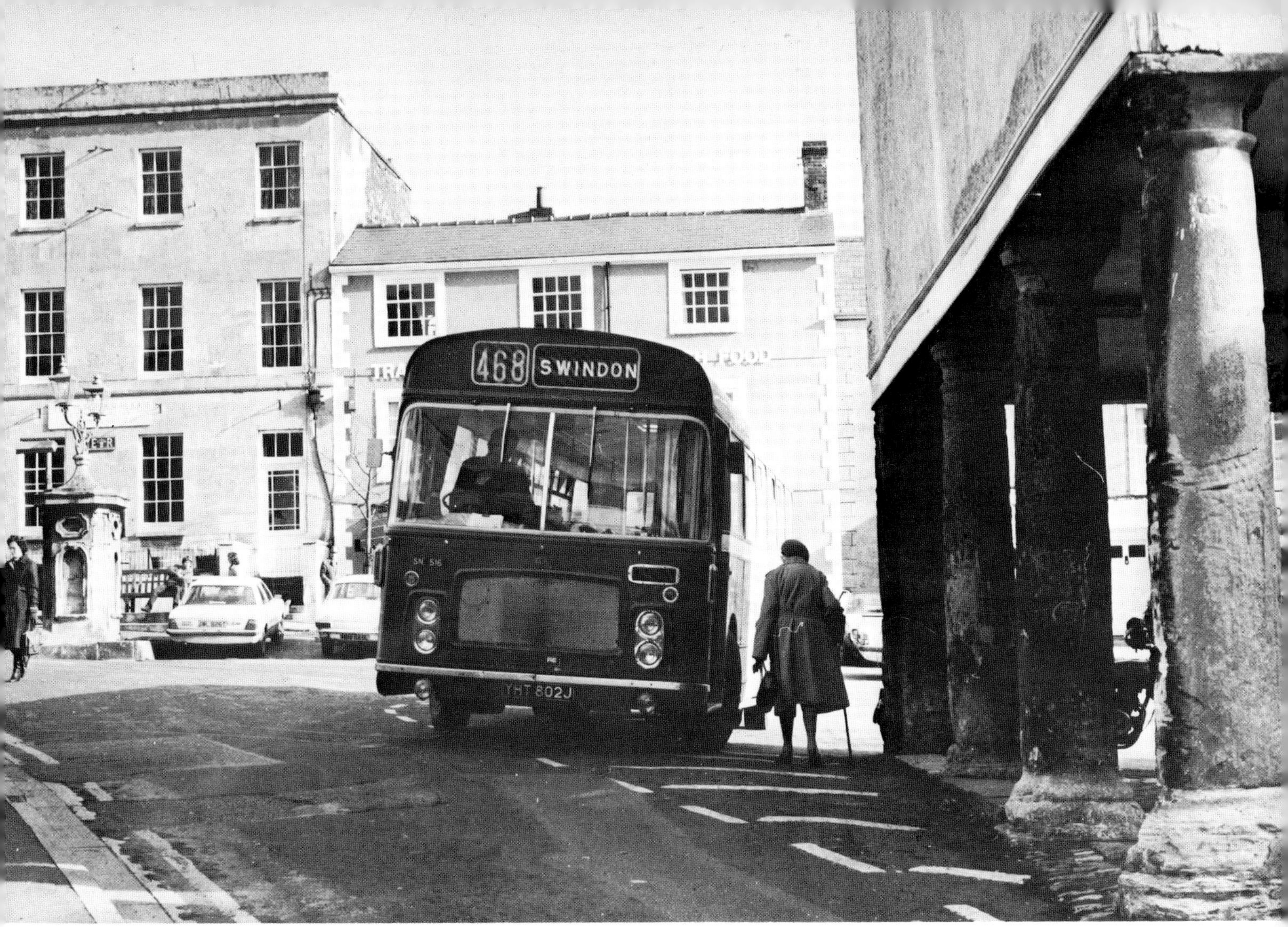
468
SWINDON
YHT 802J

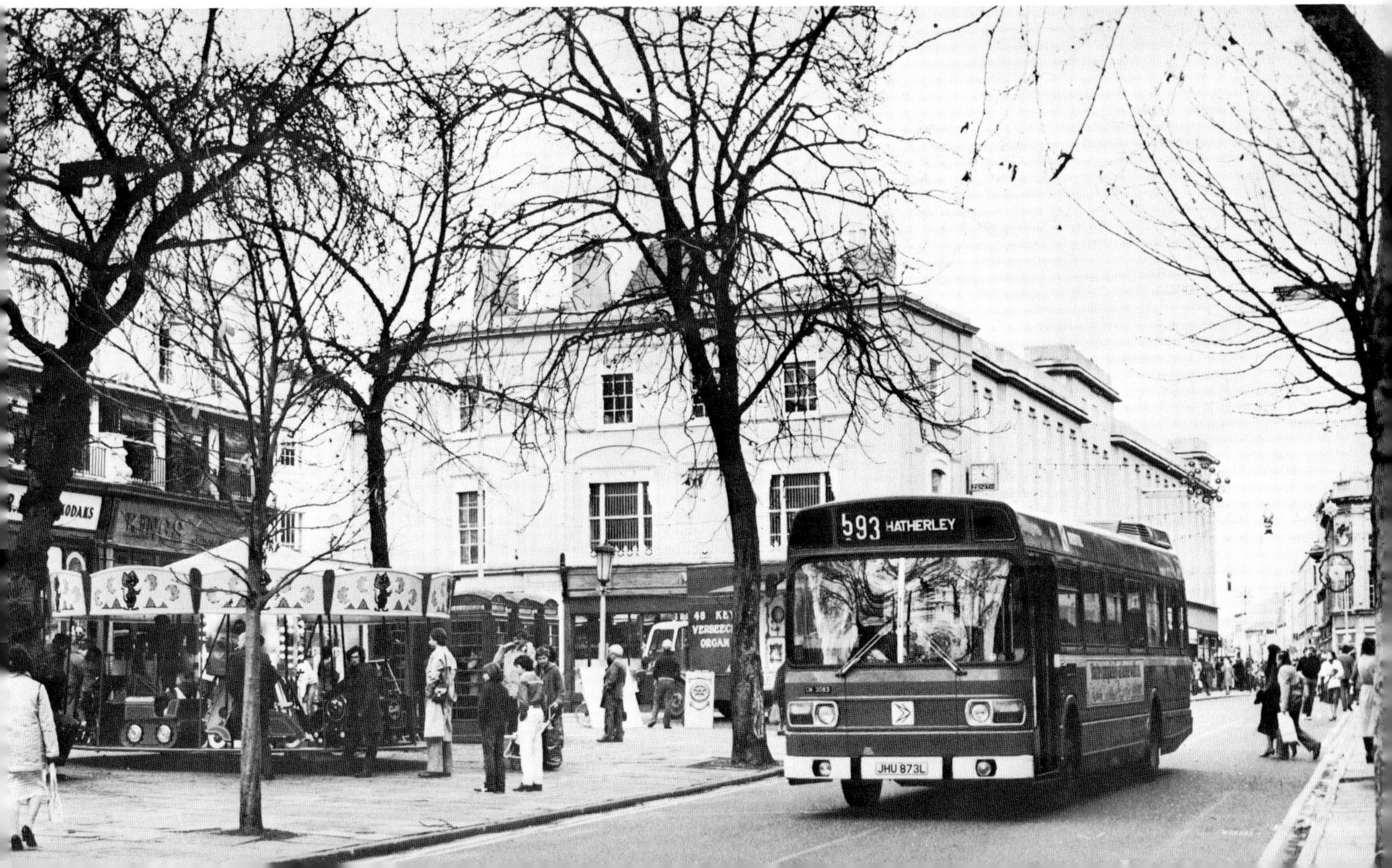
593 HATHERLEY
JHU 873L
KODAKS

Plate 19: Bristol Omnibus Co. Leyland National Mk. 2, No. CM 3506 (AAE 650V), passes slowly through the bus wash at Cheltenham garage on 23rd July 1981. This is one of the 11.6 metre versions, 30 centimetres longer than the Mk. 1 National, thus enabling the radiator to be brought from the rear to the front of the vehicle.

Rex Kennedy

Plate 20: Gloucester based Bristol REs with curved windscreens wait in line before continuing their local services. Bristol Omnibus Co. vehicles, No. 1333 (OAE 955M) and 1206 (YHY 586J) carry differing prefixes to their fleet numbers, 'GR' and 'GRG', both being allocated to Gloucester garage. The prefix GRG used on Gloucester City buses has been discontinued, although some vehicles can still be seen with these letters. Buses used on these routes now also carry GR before their numbers. Vehicles allocated to this city carry the word 'Gloucester' and the city crest in place of the word 'Bristol'.

Andrew Kennedy

Plate 21: One of the more attractive designs in the Bristol Omnibus Co. fleet, is the 1968 dual purpose 45 seat version of the Bristol RELH with ECW bodywork. Swindon allocated No. 2083 (NHW 312F) awaits departure from Malmesbury for Swindon. During 1981 these vehicles were also used on the Swindon to Oxford route.

Graham Wise

CROSVILLE

Plate 22: 'South Cheshire' was the local identity name introduced on 23rd November 1980 on Crosville vehicles in the Crewe area. On 27th November 1981, a 1972 dual-doored Crosville Leyland National, fitted with the longer earlier pod, No. SNL819 (WFM 819L), loads at Crewe bus station in preparation to take out an afternoon service. This particular vehicle was one of the first batch of Leyland Nationals delivered to Crosville, all fitted with semi-automatic gear boxes. This side view shows clearly the dual-door arrangement to avoid congestion of passengers boarding and alighting from this type of vehicle.

Rex Kennedy

Plate 23: Differing from the original designed versions by the omission of the roof pod, the 'Economy' Series 'B' Leyland National was introduced in 1978, and in July 1981, Crosville's No. SNL670 (GMB 670T), a 1978 model, passes, on a local service, one of the many Tudor buildings in the City of Chester. The city streets in Chester, follow the basic patterns introduced here by the Romans, with galleries of shops overlooking the main streets. Chester City Transport, a small municipal operator of just over fifty vehicles, share with Crosville the local services. The City Transport have operated a bus service in Chester since 1930 when the entire tram system in the town was withdrawn.

Geoff Coxon

Lodekkas

Plate 24: A fine trio of vehicles now withdrawn from the passenger carrying Crosville fleet, stand in Birkenhead garage on 29th August 1981. No. G792 (XFM 203), a Bristol LD built in 1955 with ECW bodywork, now a driver training vehicle, once carried the fleet number DLG792. When this vehicle was originally taken out of service in 1974, it was not only used as a training vehicle but as a tree lopper, having had its front dome removed. As can be seen in this view, the front dome has since been replaced, the vehicle no longer being used for tree lopping. The Bristol LD (low-height double decker) entered full production in 1954 after six pre-production models had been tried out by six different now NBC, operators, including Crosville. Earlier Lodekkas were fitted with extended front wings with louvre ventilation to keep the front brakes cool, and carried slightly deeper radiators. Between the two double deckers in this view, is Crosville recovery vehicle (DFM 208C), a 1965 Bristol MW (ex-SMG539). The Bristol MW was introduced in 1957 to replace the LS, and owing to its slightly heavier body was called the MW (medium weight). Crosville was a prolific user of this design and all production models were fitted with Gardner engines. The MW in this view was withdrawn from service in July 1979. The final vehicle in the trio, No. G166 (CFM 901C), is a Bristol FS (ex-DFG166), and is one of 127 operated by Crosville since 1960, being similar in seating design to the LD. The FS Lodekkas operated by Crosville had manually operated rear platform doors, although other operators used FS Lodekkas without doors.

Rex Kennedy

Plate 25: A 1958 Crosville Bristol LD open-top double decker, No. DLG946 (928 CFM), commemorating '50 Years of Crosville in Sunny Rhyl', leaves Prestatyn bus station for Pensarn on 22nd June 1981. Now in the white livery, this vehicle was converted to an open-topper in the late 1970s. This North Wales open-top service operates along the coast from Prestatyn at the eastern end, to Pensarn in the west, passing through Rhyl en route.

Colin Caddy

Plate 27: Liverpool City Centre sees the mingling of NBC Crosville and Ribble vehicles, together with Merseyside PTE buses. On 17th November 1981, a Crosville Bristol VR, No. DVG278 (MDM 278P), continues its journey to Rainhill as it passes through the City Centre followed by Merseyside PTE 1972 Leyland Atlantean, No. 1238 (BKC 238K), with Alexander bodywork. Liverpool's Crosville garage is the largest in the Crosville network with more than 100 vehicles allocated. The vehicle pictured here, in addition to the NBC logo, carries the local PTE crest.

Rex Kennedy

Plate 28: Chester houses the head office and works of Crosville Motor Services, and the garage, pictured here, is situated on the Liverpool Road. On 29th August 1981, a 1970 Northern Counties bodied Daimler Fleetline, No. HDG907 (TCD 377J), an ex-Southdown vehicle, stood at this garage. This vehicle was one of thirty Daimler Fleetlines, fifteen with Northern Counties bodies and fifteen with ECW bodies, acquired from Southdown in 1980, their Southdown numbers being 370 to 399.

Rex Kennedy

Plate 29: Another ex-Southdown Daimler Fleetline, this time with ECW bodywork, arrives at the Pass of Llanberis in Snowdonia, preparing to return to Caernarfon on 17th July 1981. The name 'Sherpa', which appears on Crosville vehicles operating in this part of North Wales, is clearly displayed on the front of the vehicle. No. HDL919 (XUF 389K), ex-Southdown No. 389 seen here, was allocated to Bangor garage on acquisition from Southdown in 1980, and is a highbridge type double decker indicated by the letter 'H' within the fleet number.

Geoff Mills

Plate 26: On 29th August 1981, a Crosville Bristol FS, No. DFG220 (JFM 220D) bearing the 'Wrexham' local identity name introduced in November 1980, stands in the vicinity of Runcorn garage. The infamous figure of eight Runcorn Busway incorporates the garage location en route to set down and pick up passengers. This busway gives good access to this new town and traffic-free travel for the Crosville vehicles. The 1966 vehicle pictured here was transferred to Wrexham garage from Rhyl in November 1980, and was one of the last batch of Bristol FS Lodekkas to be delivered to Crosville.

Rex Kennedy

Plate 30: A Seddon RU fitted with Seddon Pennine bodywork is one of the more unusual vehicles in the NBC network. In 1971 and 1972, Crosville purchased 100 of these vehicles, fifty being designated EPG and the remainder SPG. Crosville operate a unique fleet numbering system consisting of three letters preceeding the actual fleet number. The first letter represents the body type: e.g. S (single deck bus), E (dual purpose) etc., the second letter indicates the chassis type: e.g. R (Bristol RE), P (Seddon RU), N (Leyland National) etc., and the third letter covering the engine type: e.g. G (Gardner), B (Bristol), L (Leyland) etc. No. EPG735 (OFM 735K) was to be seen at Birkenhead garage on 29th August 1981 in dual purpose livery. These Seddon vehicles are now in the course of withdrawal from the Crosville fleet.

Rex Kennedy

Plate 31: Arriving at Caernarfon on a 'Snowdon Sherpa' service from Llanberis, Crosville Bristol LH, No. SLL635 (OCA 635P), approaches its terminus on 13th July 1981. This vehicle was one of forty fitted with Leyland engines delivered in 1975/6. The original batch of Bristol LH saloons delivered to Crosville in 1969, sixteen in total, were fitted with Perkins engines and designated SLP. By 1980 all these Perkins engined vehicles had been withdrawn.

Geoff Mills

Plate 32: The name 'De Cambria' meaning South Cambrian, seen on Crosville's Plaxton bodied Leyland Leopard No. ELL317 (RMA 317P) denotes vehicle allocation to the Aberystwyth area covering an area from Machynlleth in the north to Newcastle Emlyn in the south. This vehicle is seen swinging round to take up position in one of the bays at Cheltenham coach station on 24th August 1981, in preparation to return to Aberystwyth, having just completed refuelling. Until May 1980, No. ELL317 carried the fleet number CLL317 having changed from coach status to dual purpose.

Rex Kennedy

Plate 33: Seen resplendent in the new Crosville dual purpose livery of dark green, lime green and white, a Willowbrook bodied Leyland Leopard, No. ELL24 (DDM 24X), delivered to Crosville on 12th August 1981, stands in the garage area at Crewe on 27th November 1981. This vehicle carries the small 'Lynx' logo near the Crosville fleet-name which differs considerably in size from the logo on the vehicle pictured below at Chester.
Rex Kennedy

Plate 34: The smaller version of the Crosville 'Lynx' logo as seen on No. ELL24.
Andrew Kennedy

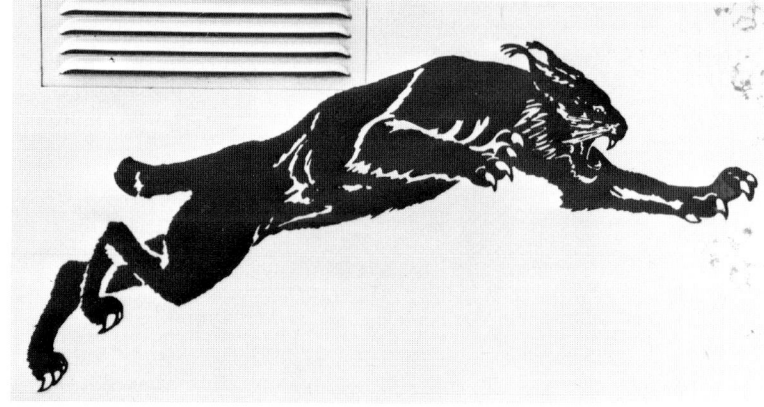

Plate 35: Crosville's 'Town Lynx' livery is seen carried by a Leyland Leopard coach, No. ELL502 (OMA 502V), fitted with Duple Dominant Mk. 2 bodywork, as it departs from Chester bus station for Nantwich on 15th July 1981. Only two vehicles carry this special livery for the 'Town Lynx' X1 and X2 services operating from Queensferry to Runcorn, Flint and Mold, the other vehicle being No. ELL503 of similar design. The livery is another combination of the colours named in the caption which accompanies **Plate 33** with the large 'Lynx' in black. A very small 'Lynx' can be seen below the windscreen.
Geoff Mills

CUMBERLAND

Plate 36: Keswick bus station is set amongst some of the finest scenery in Britain, being overlooked by the 3,054ft. lakeland mountain peak, Skiddaw. From this location Cumberland services run west to Workington and Whitehaven and east to Penrith. The bus station and garage, whose Cumberland allocation consists of under ten vehicles, are situated together, and in July 1981, a 1980 extra lowbridge 13ft. 5in. Cumberland Bristol VR, No. 426 (FAO 426V), awaits departure for Whitehaven. A Series 'B' type Leyland National, one of fifteen operated by Cumberland Motor Services, completes the scene.

Geoff Coxon

Plate 38: One of four ex-Trent 40 seat Plaxton bodied Leyland Leopards built in 1974 and acquired by Cumberland, from Trent, in 1980 is No. 609 (ACH 144H). Whilst in the Trent fleet, these vehicles were numbered 41 to 44 and are the only dual purpose coach designed vehicles in the Cumberland fleet. No. 609 is pictured in December 1981, in Whitehaven, on a Drigg service. During 1981, Cumberland Motor Services faced serious competition from the yellow buses of Yeowarts in Whitehaven on the town service. This resulted in the local identity name 'Haven Link' eventually appearing on Cumberland buses in Whitehaven, supposedly to drum up more custom in the town now competition involving a price war has crept in. Unfortunately, certain country services have been withdrawn by Cumberland Motor Services due to the loss of revenue in Whitehaven.
Peter W. Robinson

Plate 39: A dual purpose Bristol RELL, No. 297 (DAO 297K), of the Cumberland fleet, passes through Aspatria, between Maryport and Wigton, with a Carlisle to Whitehaven No. 30 service in December 1981. Within the entire Cumberland fleet of approximately 160 vehicles, almost one third are ECW bodied Bristol RELL vehicles. The allocation of the fleet is spread over six garages, the largest, by far, being Whitehaven with approximately 75 vehicles, and the smallest being Millom with only six.
Peter W. Robinson

Plate 40: A 1978 Duple bodied Leyland Leopard coach, No. 621 (VRM 621S), of the Cumberland fleet, pulls out from the line of coaches at Battersea Wharf, London on 5th December 1981. This vehicle is fitted with Grant doors which are clearly visible. Certain vehicles in the Cumberland coach fleet have the distinction of being named and fall into two categories; those with the prefix 'Lady' as in *Lady Betty* and others in the 'River' series like *River Cocker*. Battersea Wharf is used for the parking of vehicles after arriving at Victoria coach station on service. This area can accommodate up to 200 vehicles, offering a large variety of coach design on view in one place.
Geoff Mills

Plate 37: By the end of 1980 the last eight Bristol FLFs in the Cumberland fleet had been withdrawn from service. However, three of these popular vehicles, Nos. 535 (HRM 535D), 506 (507 BRM) and 534 (HRM 534D) could be seen at Wigton garage on 30th July 1981 still carrying the Cumberland name and NBC logo. Nos. 534 and 535 were withdrawn from passenger carrying service in November 1980 and No. 506 a few months earlier. Cumberland have operated 31 of these Lodekka type vehicles over the 20 years since 1960 which represents just under 2% of the entire FLF production of 1,867 vehicles.
Ian Kennedy

EASTERN COUNTIES

Plate 41: At Cambridge in 1981, the pleasurable sight of Bristol FLFs on service was still possible. In total, Eastern Counties have run 99 of these vehicles over a period of time and, No. FLF465 (KAH 465D), a 1966 model prepares to pass the garage on its way out of the town centre on a local service in January 1981. Some of the Bristol FLFs have outlived Bristol VRs brought into the Eastern Counties fleet long after them, and it is hoped we shall have the pleasure of seeing these popular vehicles on service for a few more years.
Kevin Lane

Plate 42: Eastern Counties Bristol RELL6G, No. RL519 (HPW 519L), carrying ECW bodywork, awaits departure from Drummer Street bus station, Cambridge on 25th November 1981. This bus station was opened in 1925, has since been enlarged and is the main Cambridge terminus despite efforts to find a new site. Behind this vehicle stands a Premier Travel coach in its two-tone blue livery, a regular sight at Drummer Street. This company also operates services in the area.
Rex Kennedy

Plate 43: Colchester bus station is predominantly Eastern National territory, but Eastern Counties services also work into this location. On Wednesday, 25th November 1981, a 13 ft. 8 in. Bristol VR, No. VR275 (TAH 275W) picks up more passengers soon after arrival before taking out its next service. The other Bristol VR in view is a later 1981 model, No. 3127 (XHK 232X) of the Eastern National fleet. The bus station itself sits below a multi-storey car-park.
Rex Kennedy

Plate 44: Open-top buses were withdrawn from the Eastern Counties fleet in 1971, and were not used again until seven years later when one was hired from Western National for sea front duties between Sheringham and Overstrand. No. OT1 (VDV 752) acquired from Western National in 1979, is a 1957 long wheelbase Bristol LDL6G with ECW bodywork, and is seen at Cromer on 1st August 1981 in the red and white livery. When owned by Western National this vehicle carried the fleet No. 1935, and was one of two, together with No. 1936 (VDV 753), fitted with 37 seats on the upper deck and 33 seats on the lower. No. 1936 is also now in the Eastern Counties fleet as open-topper No. OT2.
Geoff Mills

Plate 45: A pair of Eastern Counties 1963 Bristol FS/ECW Lodekkas stand at Great Yarmouth in the summer of 1981, headed by No. LFS52 (52 CPW). Both vehicles carry the 'Golden Jubilee' stickers behind the company name. These two Lodekkas are of the short wheelbase variety, differing externally from the long wheelbase type seen in the previous picture, which carries an extra small window at the rear of the bus. The Bristol FS of course, also differs from the FLF in having the rear entrance. No. LFS52 was withdrawn from the fleet in September 1981.
Kevin Lane

Plate 46: In full white coach livery, Eastern Counties No. RLE747 (GCL 349N), a 1974 Bristol RELH6L with ECW bodywork makes its way through the busy Great Yarmouth streets in the summer of 1981. This vehicle is a dual purpose 49 seater OMO version and is powered by the Gardner 6HLX engine which replaced a Leyland 0680 engine in February 1981. Other RELHs in this batch have been scheduled for conversion in this manner. Another engine conversion in the Eastern Counties fleet was made to Leyland National Mk. 1, No. LN781 (DPW 781T) when fitted with a Gardner engine and renumbered LG781. This vehicle is instantly recognisable by its protruding front end.

Kevin Lane

EASTERN COUNTIES
50 YEARS OF PUBLIC TRANSPORT
GOLDEN JUBILEE
1931 1981

Plate 47: Ford Transit 16 seater 'Community Bus' with Mellor Coachcraft bodywork, No. MB994 (OVF 994W), is one of the minibuses operated by Eastern Counties. The 16 seat version seems to have taken over from the 12 seater model, which was first introduced when the idea of these smaller vehicles being used on rural routes through local villages, came into force at Sharrington in 1975. The services are backed by the local council with the local residents providing volunteer drivers trained by Eastern Counties. No. MB994, pictured at King's Lynn on 30th May 1981, was delivered new in July 1980 and was originally painted dark red, but was repainted in the NBC white livery, with a red roof, in September 1980.

Geoff Mills

Plate 48: Eastern Counties 1978 Bristol VRT No. VR223 (BVG 223T) in full advertising livery of dark blue, representing The Phoenix Assurance Co. passes the city walls of Norwich on 14th October 1981. This vehicle was painted in this livery in June 1981 and is based in Norwich.

Geoff Mills

Plate 50: Passing one of the green parkland areas to be found in Cambridge, is Eastern Counties 11.6 metre Leyland National Mk. 2 No. LN619 (PEX 619W), which was brought into service in November 1980. The restyled Mk. 2 'Nationals' first entered the Eastern Counties fleet in March 1980, after Western National had taken delivery of the first Mk. 2 for NBC in 1979, one month after being featured at the Scottish show.

Rex Kennedy

Plate 49: Cambridge Eastern Counties garage houses a variety of bus designs. One of the bargain day returns, now commonly featured on the back of many NBC coaches throughout Britain advertising cheap services to London from all parts of the NBC network, is clearly portrayed on an Eastern Counties Leyland Leopard No. LL794 (OEX 794W). Other vehicles in attendance on 25th November 1981, are Leyland National Mk. 1 No. LN551 (OAH 551M), Bristol RELH No. RE850 (SAH 850M) and dual purpose Bristol RELL No. RLE861 (WNG 861H). This scene shows four styles of bodywork from differing manufacturers and from left to right are Willowbrook, Leyland, Plaxton and ECW.
Rex Kennedy

Plate 51: Proceeding down the High Street towards the bus station at Halstead, Eastern National Mk. 2 Leyland National, No. 1926 (MHJ 722V), carrying the Halstead garage code, passes the Premier Travel Agency on 25th November 1981. The all-green livery is carried by this vehicle which is fitted with the heating and ventilation pod.

Rex Kennedy

Plate 52: Eastern National 1967 Bristol FLF No. 2895 (WNO 983F), based at the London Road, Southend garage, is seen on service in Romford, Essex on 8th April 1981. On 1st January 1964, the Eastern National fleet contained 91 Bristol FLF buses and six FLF coaches. By November 1980, FLFs still numbered 79, with four FLF open-toppers, in total almost equalling the Bristol VR allocation of the Eastern National fleet. Sadly no FLFs now remain in the service fleet, apart from open-toppers. No. 2895, pictured here, was de-licenced in June 1981.

Dave Savage

Plate 53: Bishop's Stortford based Ford R1014 single decker, No. 1004 (MAR 779P), fitted with 43 seat Duple Dominant bodywork, was one of a batch of five of this design delivered to Eastern National in 1976 and numbered 1000–1004. All five, since delivery, have operated from Bishop's Stortford garage. The next delivery of vehicles of a compatible size, Bristol LHs, did not arrive until 1977. No. 1004 pictured at Stanstead, Essex on 19th August 1981, was withdrawn in November 1981 and sold to a dealer in Sherburn in Elmet in Yorkshire, together with the remaining four. A comparatively short life with Eastern National.

Geoff Mills

Plate 54: Colchester bus station sees a variety of bus and coach design and is situated adjacent to the Eastern National garage in the centre of the town. Arrivals and departures are constant, and 'off duty' buses are also parked at this location. On Wednesday, 25th November 1981, a 53 seater Eastern National Bristol RELL6G, with ECW bodywork, No. 1517 (FWC 440H), picks up passengers before proceeding to Maldon. Colchester, of course, has its own 'Corporation' fleet, which also uses this bus station, the existence of this municipal operator resulting in the comparatively small allocation of Eastern National vehicles to Colchester garage.

Andrew Kennedy

Plate 55: Two Eastern National vehicles prepare to leave their prospective stops at Brentwood in November 1981. Both are Brentwood based, a garage with an allocation similar to Colchester in total. No. 1531 (MHK 913J), a ten year old Bristol RELL6G with the curved windscreen, in the all-over leaf green livery, waits with a 1981 Bristol VRT No. 3092 (STW 36W). Both vehicles carry ECW bodywork.
Kevin Lane

Plate 56: In the vicinity of the University of Essex buildings at Wivenhoe, an Eastern National Bedford YMQ, No. 1050 (TJN 973W), with Wadham Stringer Vanguard bodywork, picks up a fare from a bleak joint Eastern National & National Express bus and coach stop on 9th December 1981, during the very cold spell of weather which was experienced, at that time, throughout Britain. This vehicle is fitted with the dual purpose 34 high-backed coach seats, as against 33 seats which was the original intention. The bus is en route for Clacton, its home base.
Geoff Mills

Plate 57: An Eastern National 1972 Bristol RELH6G, with ECW bodywork, No. 1404 (VHK 177L), was returned, for rebuilding, to Eastern Coachworks, Lowestoft. It arrived back at Eastern National in June 1981 with re-designed front and rear ends, and was refurbished in a new livery of white, with red and blue bands and a black skirt. This new design bodywork is the prototype for forthcoming ECW coaches and the vehicle is pictured in Colchester on 2nd October 1981.
Geoff Mills

Plate 58: Halstead garage, one of the smallest in the Eastern National territory both in size and allocation, houses both double and single deck designs. On 25th November 1981, an Eastern National 1975 Bristol VR, No. 3059 (LJN 654P), allocated to this garage, pulls away, leaving at the entrance, a 1972 Bristol RE, No. 1544 (RPU 884K), which is also Halstead based. The red brick premises at Halstead are of an attractive design with the company name prominently displayed. On this day, a 1966 Bristol FLF was to be found, withdrawn from service, at the rear of the garage.
Rex Kennedy

EAST KENT

Plate 59: The picturesque town of Tenterden provides an interesting background for East Kent Leyland Atlantean with ECW bodywork No. 7008 (JJG 8P). This vehicle was one of fifteen delivered in 1976, these being the first new double deckers to enter the East Kent fleet for seven years. It prepares to leave for Canterbury on 23rd November 1981.

Rex Kennedy

Plate 60: Leyland National Mk. 1, No. 1120 (MFN 120R), of the East Kent fleet, passes through the Kent village of Thannington Without en route for Canterbury bus station, on 23rd November 1981. No. 1120 was one of the 'Nationals' which escaped the fate of being sold by East Kent to other NBC subsidiaries such as South Wales and National Welsh, during 1981. This action was the result of service revisions, which then left East Kent with vehicles surplus to requirements.

Andrew Kennedy

Plate 61: White roofed dual purpose East Kent Leyland National Mk. 1, No. 1082 (NFN 82R), pulls away from Canterbury shopping centre on 23rd November 1981. This 11.3 metre model is fitted with 48 high backed seats, and was originally destined, with others delivered at the same time, for cross country services which never materialised.

Rex Kennedy

Plate 62: Three designs of East Kent double decker are at the back of Ashford garage on 23rd November 1981. The AEC Regent V, No. 7758 (GJG 758D), with Park Royal bodywork, in the foreground, was delivered to East Kent in 1966, and was one of the largest batch of Regent Vs' bought by East Kent since 1959. In the centre of the trio is No. 7571 (571 RKJ), a 1961 Leyland PDR1/1 Mk. 2 with Metro-Cammell bodywork (ex-Maidstone & District No. 5571). This was one of four vehicles transferred, in 1974, from the Maidstone & District fleet, which had previously been on loan to East Kent after services at Ashford had been taken over from Maidstone & District by East Kent in 1973. The remaining three vehicles involved were Nos. 7572, 7575 and 7585, their Maidstone & District numbers being 5572, 5575 and 5585. Furthest away at the back of the garage is East Kent No. 7009 (JJG 9P), a 1976 Leyland Atlantean with ECW bodywork, one of fifteen of this type in the East Kent fleet. Ashford garage itself was, of course, once Maidstone & District property.

Rex Kennedy

Plate 63: East Kent's AEC Regent V double deckers were being phased out during 1981, and time is now fast running out for these very popular AEC vehicles. Pictured at Dover on 7th July 1981, was No. 7939 (MFN 939F), one of the last batch delivered to The East Kent Road Car Co. in late 1967. The vehicles in this batch were wider than the earlier deliveries and represented one of the last orders received by Park Royal for this type of vehicle. East Kent, since the introduction of the 'Regents' in 1959, had taken no less than 161 of these vehicles, which were succeeded by Daimler Fleetlines.

Dave Savage

Plate 64: An Isle of Thanet open-top bus works its way along the sea front at Margate on 16th August 1981. This 1963 Leyland Atlantean Mk. 2 (620 UKM), with Weymann bodywork, started its life in the Maidstone & District fleet as No. DH 620, indicating a highbridge double decker. Whilst carrying its second fleet number 5620 for Maidstone & District, it was converted to open-top in June 1981 and again renumbered 0620, and was a welcome sight in 1981 on the Thanet coast in its new appealing form. However, the vehicle, although bearing the East Kent fleetname, is only on loan from Maidstone & District. Its route, as indicated on the side of the bus, covers 16 miles of coastline from Pegwell Bay to Minnis Bay with an hourly service.

Dave Savage

Plate 65: Beneath the watchful eye of Dover Castle, an ex-Southdown 1971 Daimler Fleetline, No. 7325 (VUF 325K), now in the East Kent fleet, with Northern Counties bodywork, proudly shows off her attractive P & O Ferries light blue and white livery. Two other vehicles in this livery are Nos. 7324 and 7326, also ex-Southdown. These vehicles once carried Southdown numbers 2124–2126 and are now allocated to Dover East Kent garage operating the P & O courtesy service at Dover.

Dave Savage

Plate 66: An AEC Swift, with Marshall bodywork, No. 1200 (RJG 200G), of the East Kent fleet, picks up passengers alongside Canterbury bus station on 23rd November 1981. This 51 seater 'Swift' was built in 1969 and the white panel below the windows once carried the original East Kent fleetname prior to the introduction of the NBC corporate liveries in 1972.

Rex Kennedy

Plate 67: East Kent Willowbrook bodied Bristol VRT, No. 7989 (TFN 989T), turns at Margate on Easter Monday 1981. The Bristol VRT appeared for the first time in the East Kent fleet in 1976, and the Willowbrook body makes an interesting change to the more common ECW bodywork of the VR range. This particular vehicle was one of the last batch of Willowbrook VRs delivered to this company.

Kevin Lane

Plate 68: A single deck dual-doored East Kent Daimler Fleetline, No. 1805 (SKO 805H), with Marshall bodywork and sporting the special 'Seaspeed' livery of white with red and blue bands, is seen at Dover on 7th July 1981. This vehicle is one of eight East Kent buses acquired from Maidstone & District during 1976/77, four being painted in this livery and four in 'Sealink' livery. The 'Seaspeed' vehicles are used on contract services from Dover Priory station to the Dover hoverport.

Dave Savage

Plate 69: A combined East Kent/Maidstone & District 'coach travel' advertiser sets down passengers at Margate on 16th August 1981. This East Kent vehicle, No. 7651 (XJJ 651V), a Bristol VRT with an ECW body, is one of two in this livery, a similar one being operated by Maidstone & District.
Dave Savage

Plate 70: A 1974 East Kent AEC Reliance with Duple coachwork, pulls into Canterbury bus station on 23rd November 1981. No. 8790 (PFN 790M) is en route for Ramsgate. A total commitment by East Kent to the AEC chassis began in 1955 with the 'Reliance' saloons, and many AECs remain in the fleet today. No. 8790 once carried the Townsend Thoresen livery of basically orange and white, but she is seen here in the customary NBC coach white.
Rex Kennedy

EAST MIDLAND MANSFIELD

Plate 71: A general view overlooking Mansfield bus station, which was opened on 20th November 1977, as Mansfield/East Midland 1978 Leyland National Mk. 1, No. 609 (BAL 609T), backs away from the pick up point before leaving on 26th November 1981. Three Bristol VRs complete the scene. Mansfield District is a subsidiary company of East Midland, and from December 1980, buses allocated to Mansfield garage started to receive the fleetname 'Mansfield', dropping the word 'District' they had previously carried. This particular bus station also caters for Trent bus services, Mansfield being one of the few towns housing two garages of differing NBC operators.
Rex Kennedy

Plate 72: Mansfield & District 1967 Bristol FLF Lodekka, with Gardner 8.4 litre engine, No. 484 (SRB 60F), resplendent in the original green and cream Mansfield & District livery, takes the Mansfield town ring road on service on 26th November 1981. This vehicle was originally owned by Midland General who were amalgamated with Mansfield & District Traction Co. However, since 1977, Midland General has been amalgamated with the Trent NBC fleet.
Rex Kennedy

Plate 73: The East Midland/Mansfield garage at Sutton Road, Mansfield is by no means small. A 1974 Leyland Leopard with Duple coachwork, No. 3 (NNN 3M), waits beside the wash on 29th July 1981 and carries the combined fleetnames.
Rex Kennedy

Plate 74: Bearing the dual-purpose livery, East Midland/Mansfield 1976 Leyland Leopard with Alexander 'T' type bodywork, No. 9 (PRA 9R), is seen parked in Mansfield on 26th November 1981. The 'T' prototype first saw the light of day at the 1974 Commercial Show, but production did not commence on this design until 1976. Other NBC companies operating the Alexander 'T' type include Trent, West Riding, Yorkshire Traction and United Counties. This particular vehicle carries the name 'East Midland' above Mansfield in the fleetname, whereas when coaches carried the words 'Mansfield District' together with East Midland, the names were often in reverse order.
Rex Kennedy

Plate 75: Leaving London's Victoria coach station for Liverpool on 25th June 1981 is East Midland/Mansfield Leyland Leopard coach, No. 98 (YCH 898M), with 40 seat Plaxton bodywork. Nos. 98 and 99 are ex-Trent vehicles and were withdrawn from service by them in October 1980 where they carried the fleet numbers 37 and 38. These vehicles were acquired by East Midland in December 1980. The only other vehicle in this batch, No. 39 still remained in the Trent fleet at the end of 1981.
Dave Savage

Plate 76: Twenty four years after originally entering service for East Midland, No. T2 (WAL 123), a Leyland Titan lowbridge PD3/4 with Weymann bodywork, now a driver training vehicle, passes through Sheffield city centre on 19th April 1981. This vehicle originally carried the fleet number D123, and East Midland, in fact, were one of the first companies to purchase the lowbridge PD3/4 models with Weymann bodywork, being one of the few English operators still requesting the 'lowbridge' design at the time.
Adrian Foster

Plate 77: On 26th November 1981, an East Midland Leyland National Mk. 2, No. 622 (MWG 622X), slowly enters the small bus station in Matlock, Derbyshire approximately three months after entering service with East Midland. This location is predominantly used by Trent vehicles for the NBC and also by the independent operator, Hulley's.
Andrew Kennedy

Plate 78: This interesting all-over advertising bus is in red and yellow livery, and is one of three Leyland Nationals in the East Midland fleet carrying this livery. No. 575 (XRR 575M), together with No. 584 was painted in this Baskill's advertising livery in February 1980 and No. 573 followed later. All three vehicles were once dual-doored and were converted to front entrance only, with all other dual-door Leyland Nationals in the East Midland fleet over a period of time being treated similarly, changing the seating capacity from 44 to 49 seats. On 19th April 1981 No. 575 awaits departure for Gainsborough at Pond Street bus station, Sheffield. The municipal operator, Chesterfield Transport, also run two Leyland Nationals in a similar advertising livery.
Adrian Foster

EAST YORKSHIRE

Plate 79: East Yorkshire Bristol VRT, No. 960 (PAT 960R), with ECW Mk. 3 bodywork, passes through Hull with a service to Scarborough on 27th August 1981. East Yorkshire's fleet is predominantly double deck, and of the Bristol double deckers used in Britain the VRT appears the more popular with operators, as noise level has been considerably reduced on this model. The East Yorkshire fleet is one of the smallest in the NBC network.
Rex Kennedy

Plate 80: Standing before the brick facade of York railway station, East Yorkshire 1980 Bristol VRT, No. 517 (PAG 517W), with ECW bodywork, awaits departure for Hull. The service between Hull and York brings East Yorkshire double deckers into the West Yorkshire area. A West Yorkshire Bristol VR of similar design, bearing the YORK fleetname and city crest, waits behind, beneath the station clock on 16th September 1981.
Rex Kennedy

Plate 81: Kingston-upon-Hull sees a combination of poppy red East Yorkshire vehicles working together with the local blue and white Corporation buses. The city is worked predominantly by double deckers, and on 27th August 1981 an East Yorkshire 1969 Daimler Fleetline, No. 869 (RAT 869G), with Park Royal bodywork prepares to overtake a local Kingston-upon-Hull Transport vehicle, No. 321 (DRH 321L), a Leyland Atlantean with Roe bodywork. The East Yorkshire vehicle is fitted with the Beverley Bar tapered roof outline which was introduced to enable double deck buses to pass through Beverley Bar, the small pointed Gothic archway leading into the town of Beverley. The standard 'lowbridge' or 'highbridge' vehicles would not pass beneath this arch. However, since the town bypass has been in operation, buses no longer use the archway and from 1971 onwards, standard 'high' or 'lowbridge' buses were purchased by East Yorkshire.

Rex Kennedy

Plate 82: Two differing designs of NBC East Yorkshire double deckers lie parked at Ferensway bus park, Hull on 27th August 1981. In the foreground, 1971 Daimler Fleetline, No. 885 (WKH 885J), with Alexander bodywork, is one of the first 'highbridge' vehicles ordered by East Yorkshire after double deck vehicles no longer passed beneath Beverley Bar. This vehicle once carried the attractive dark blue and primrose livery, and was one of ten ordered at the time. Alongside No. 885 is No. 977 (WAG 977S), a standard Bristol VR built in 1977.

Rex Kennedy

Plate 83: Waiting near Victoria coach station on 25th June 1981 is No. 194 (JKH 194V), an East Yorkshire Leyland Leopard Plaxton bodied coach in white livery. Until 1981, coaches could often be found lined up at this particular point near the ex-Samuelson's garage, pending pulling in for washing before taking out their next service. This garage is now used for setting down passengers, in addition to offering bus washing and refuelling facilities at peak periods. The majority of coaches purchased by East Yorkshire carry Plaxton bodywork, the manufacturer being located at nearby Scarborough.

Dave Savage

Plate 84: A bus park used by both East Yorkshire and local municipal buses is situated between Hull Paragon railway station and Lombard Street, Kingston-upon-Hull Transport garage. This park also lies adjacent to the large covered Ferensway bus station in Hull. On 27th August 1981 an East Yorkshire Leyland National Mk. 2, without the pod, No. 200 (NAT 200V), in the all-over poppy red livery, stands off duty. This vehicle is one of the longer 11.6 metre models fitted with 49 seats.

Rex Kennedy

Plate 85: An East Yorkshire 1972 Leyland Leopard PSU5, No. 196 (KGJ 475K), with Plaxton coachwork and fitted with 57 seats, is seen at Lincoln on 25th August 1981. In 1980, this coach was in the United Automobile fleet as No. 1097, having been acquired by them in 1978 from National Travel (South East), previously being in the Samuelsons fleet. During 1978, National Travel (South East) became National Travel (London).

Geoff Mills

Plate 86: Overlooked by the statue of King Alfred at Winchester, Hants & Dorset Leyland National Mk. 1, No. 3634 (GFX 973N), carrying the orange and blue 'Wintonline' fleetname, pulls away after picking up passengers on a sunny 19th November 1981. The name 'Wintonline' indicates allocation to Winchester garage, the local identity being introduced on 27th January 1980 as a result of an M.A.P. survey.

Rex Kennedy

Plate 87: Hants & Dorset 1979 Bristol VRT, No. 3407 (BFX 575T), is seen on service at Bournemouth on 5th December 1981. The 'South Wessex' fleetname was introduced into the East Dorset area as a result of an M.A.P. Survey. This effected the closure of the Hants & Dorset garage in Norwich Avenue, Bournemouth on 29th November 1980.

Andrew Kennedy

Plate 88: Preparing to leave for Andover from Salisbury bus station on 13th October 1981, is a Hants & Dorset 1976 Bristol VRT, No. 3346 (NEL 120P), fitted with coach seating. Six vehicles of this type are in the Hants & Dorset fleet and all are allocated to Andover and Southampton garages, this particular one bearing the fleetname 'Antonbus' is based at Andover. Salisbury is one of the busiest centres for Hants & Dorset vehicles, and was once Wilts & Dorset territory prior to the amalgamation of the two companies in 1972.

Rex Kennedy

Plate 90: A busy vehicle ferry in the summer season, the Shell Bay to Sandbanks ferry, conveys the Swanage to Bournemouth service across Poole Bay. Only certain Hants & Dorset buses are able to negotiate the dip as the vehicle proceeds on to the ferry, and the cut-away section at the front of the Hants & Dorset Bristol LH, to deal with this problem is very apparent. The vehicle is No. 3534 (ORU 534M), a 1974 model pictured in June 1981 at Shell Bay. A batch of ten Bristol LHs with cut-away fronts, numbered 3530 to 3539, were adapted in this manner for this service.

Kevin Lane

Plate 89: The exit to the bus station at Winchester proudly displays the Hants & Dorset company name, as a 1978 Bristol VR of this company, No. 3396 (YEL 3T), leaves on service on 13th October 1981. 'Wintonline' and the colour codes above the fleet number, of one yellow and one orange spot, denote the vehicle's home base as being Winchester, and 'Wintonline' the local identity fleetname, is derived from the ancient name of the city. A Bristol VR, with coach seating, from Southampton garage portraying the fleetname 'South Hants' waits at the exit. This bus station is also the site of the Hants & Dorset garage. The now closed ex-King Alfred garage, the company absorbed into Hants & Dorset in 1973, was approximately 400 yards along the road.
Rex Kennedy

Plate 91: Hants & Dorset Leyland National Mk. 1 'Advertiser' No. 3714 (VFX 980S), stands outside its home garage of Southampton on Sunday 4th October 1981. The livery, which advertises Hants & Dorset season tickets, is two-tone green with a white roof.
Andrew Kennedy

Plate 92: Hants & Dorset had withdrawn all Bristol FLF Lodekkas from service by 1981. No. 1255 (KRU 225F), with fleet number obliterated, stands near Eastleigh garage and works on 24th May 1981. Hants & Dorset had in its fleet Bristol FLFs with Gardner, Leyland and Bristol engines, and this particular 1967 vehicle is fitted with a Bristol engine. In 1971 it carried the fleet number 1558. After being sold to a dealer in London, it was exported to the U.S.A. in November 1981 joining others exported earlier.
Andrew Kennedy

Plate 93: Dual-purpose Hants & Dorset 1970 Leyland Leopard coach, No. 1059 (SRU 999H) with 49 seat Plaxton bodywork, stands at Basingstoke bus station on Sunday 18th October 1981. This vehicle, together with No. 1061, was used on the daily X14 service and in February 1981 carried the words 'Londonlink' alongside the Hants & Dorset fleetname.
Rex Kennedy

Provincial

Plate 94: Maintenance bays at Hoeford Provincial garage on 7th November 1981, accommodate three differing types of single deckers of the Hants & Dorset 'New Provincial' fleet. No. 3555 (GLJ 487N), a Bristol LH is flanked by two Leyland Nationals, No. 3732 (WFX 257S), a dual-purpose version and No. 3659 (MJT 881P), a normal service bus. All these vehicles carry Hants & Dorset fleet numbers. Hoeford garage is shared by both this company and Provincial and was opened in October 1976, although a garage existed here in the days of the original Provincial (Gosport & Fareham) Company.
Andrew Kennedy

Plate 95: Again carrying combined fleetnames and a Hants & Dorset number, No. 1614 (NLJ 829G), a dual-purpose 50 seater Bristol RELL sporting the red and white livery, pulls away from Gosport bus station on 7th November 1981. In 1971 this Hants & Dorset vehicle carried the fleet number 840 prior to the amalgamation with Wilts & Dorset. The bus station pictured here was rebuilt in 1972 at the location known as Gosport Ferry.
Rex Kennedy

Plate 96: Hants & Dorset 1971 Bristol RE, No. 1655 (BCG 103J), skirts the traffic island adjacent to Gosport bus station on 7th November 1981. This vehicle, ex-Gosport & Fareham No. 3 in July 1980, was one of ten REs which, after an M.A.P. survey, was transferred from Provincial to the Hants & Dorset fleet and based at Fareham garage. The result of the survey took effect on 29th June 1980, with revised services and a local identity for buses from Hants & Dorset's Fareham garage, and from Provincial's Hoeford garage. The new Provincial fleetname is seen on the front of the buses and reads 'Provincial Joint Services'.
Andrew Kennedy

Plate 97: After the Market Analysis Project survey in Gosport, only two 44 seat dual-doored Bristol REs remained in service with Provincial, the others being incorporated in the Hants & Dorset fleet. No. 10 (ECG 110K), has been renumbered 100 and painted in the early post-war emerald green and cream livery commemorating 100 years of the Gosport & Fareham Omnibus Co. (1878–1978). It is pictured here on 7th November 1981 at Gosport bus station, more than three years after it was originally repainted. The other dual-doored RE, No. 12 (ECG 112K) remains in National green livery.

Andrew Kennedy

Plate 98: Parked at Hoeford garage on 7th November 1981 are three Provincial Mk. 1 Leyland Nationals, No. 14 (HOR 414L), No. 33 (JBP 133P) and in the wash, No. 25 (UAA 225M), all carrying the totally green livery. The Provincial fleet was, at this time, entirely Leyland National, with the exception of the two REs mentioned in the previous caption, and a Bristol LH No. 55 (NLJ 522M).

Andrew Kennedy

Plate 99: Leyland National Mk. 1 of the Provincial fleet, No. 30 (JBP 130P) carrying the white band beneath the windows, stands inside the old part of Hoeford garage on 7th November 1981. Only five Leyland National Mk. 1 vehicles were delivered to Provincial in 1975 of which this is one. Of the entire fleet, only the Bristol LH was not dual-doored or fitted with 44 seats. The LH was also the only vehicle not bought new by Provincial, being acquired from Hants & Dorset in 1980 and was the only vehicle fitted with 43 seats.

Rex Kennedy

Plate 101: An ex-Southdown Leyland PSU3 coach fitted with Duple bodywork, now No. 3076 (RUF 807H), in the Hants & Dorset fleet, stands in one of the Shamrock & Rambler coach parks at Bournemouth on 5th December 1981. This vehicle was acquired, in May 1981, by Hants & Dorset from Southdown where it carried the fleet number 1807.

Andrew Kennedy

Coach Fleet

Plate 100: Shamrock & Rambler coaches are regularly parked quite near to Bournemouth railway station at the rear of Holdenhurst Road. After a stormy period of weather on 19th November 1981, No. 3086 (SLJ 386X), a Leyland PSU5 fitted with Plaxton Supreme V coachwork, new to Shamrock & Rambler in October 1981, stands reflected in the aftermath of the storm with a Duple bodied AEC Reliance, No. 3029 (TFH 162R). In May 1981, Shamrock & Rambler, who up to that date were part of the National Travel (South West) fleet, became incorporated into Hants & Dorset resulting in a change in fleet numbers when their premises in Bournemouth, together with a large number of coaches, were sold to Hants & Dorset. Prior to this, No. 3029 carried the fleet number 162 when with National Travel (South West). In the days when Shamrock & Rambler were privately owned, their coaches carried names such as *Severn*, *Ajax* and *Wiltshire*.

Rex Kennedy

Plate 102: Caught by the sunlight at Bournemouth, Shamrock & Rambler Leyland PSU3 coach, No. 3021 (REL 401R), fitted with Willowbrook 'Spacecar' bodywork, is seen parked near Holdenhurst Road, Bournemouth on 5th December 1981. The 'Spacecar' design of coach in the past has been peculiar to National Travel in addition to a few other uses including Leicester City Transport. This particular vehicle was once part of the National Travel (South West) fleet and prior to its changeover to Hants & Dorset was numbered 122.

Andrew Kennedy

LINCOLNSHIRE

Plate 103: The Lincolnshire seaside resort of Skegness is graced by an open-top sea front service. Ex-Southdown Bristol FS6G, No. 2351 (XPM 42), in the Lincolnshire fleet since 1978, carrying an all-white livery, picks up more passengers at Skegness in the summer of 1981. Whilst in the Southdown fleet this vehicle carried the fleet number 2042, and prior to that, when with Brighton, Hove & District, taken over by Southdown on 1st January 1969, it carried the fleet number 42. She is now named *Lincolnshire Poacher* and a similar vehicle purchased, No. 2350 (ex-Southdown No. 2041), also from the Brighton, Hove & District fleet, now carries the name *Lincolnshire Imp*. Both vehicles were open-toppers whilst in the Brighton fleet.

Kevin Lane

Plate 104: A Lincolnshire 1980 Bristol VRT double decker, No. 1948 (LVL 803V), passes through the wash at Scunthorpe garage on 27th August 1981. The garage is situated in the same area as the covered bus station, and adjacent to the new paved shopping area. Lincolnshire's Scunthorpe garage has an approximate allocation of 40 vehicles, the majority of which, whilst not in service, are parked in the large bus park behind the wash.

Rex Kennedy

Plate 144: Malvern, with its rolling hills, is a popular inland resort for visitors in spring and summer. Services at Malvern are fewer since the closure of Malvern Midland Red garage on 1st October 1976 and vehicles used on local services operate from Worcester garage. One of the original ornate Midland Red bus shelters is seen in this view taken on 28th November 1981, as a 1976 Leyland Leopard of this company, No. 456 (JOX 456P), with Plaxton bodywork, en route for Birmingham with service X43, approaches Great Malvern from its southern terminus at Malvern Wells.

Rex Kennedy

Plate 145: The interior of Swadlincote garage on 29th July 1981 portrays two of the more prolific vehicles in the Midland Red fleet, the Leyland Nationals. Midland Red in their time have purchased well over 400 of these vehicles, more than 30 of which passed, in December 1973, to West Midlands PTE. Two 11.3 metre Mk. 1 versions, Nos. 414 (GOL 414N) and 419 (GOL 419N), are seen bearing the 'Lancer' fleetname which is familiar to Swadlincote.

Rex Kennedy

Plate 141: Standing beside the garage buildings at Nuneaton on 29th July 1981, is an ex-Midland Red LC9 coach having been cut down for use as a towing tender. Still carrying the old fleet number 5830, its registration number whilst in service was GHA 330D. This vehicle was built in 1966, and is a Leyland Leopard with Plaxton bodywork. When in service, the 36 seat LC9 coaches were used on extended coach tours, and from late 1972 were re-seated to 40 for more general coach duties. Eight more vehicles of this design are also used as recovery vehicles at various Midland Red garages. The Leyland National sitting behind the towing tender is a locally allocated 'Hunter'.
Rex Kennedy

Plate 142: Taking a rest at Pitlochry in the Scottish Highlands on 22nd June 1981, Midland Red Leyland Leopard, No. 614 (NOE 614R), with 45 seat Plaxton body, carries the 'National Holidays' transfers on the front and side. The Midland Red fleetname is obscured by a 'National Holidays' removable board. On coaches, the word 'National' is always in alternate red and blue lettering, but whenever 'National Holidays' is used, the word 'Holidays' is in all-blue lettering. The Scottish tour in progress for this vehicle is to the 'Glorious North West Highlands and Skye', a fine scenic experience for all its passengers.
Rex Kennedy

Plate 143: One of the dwindling double deck fleet of Midland Red vehicles stands in the yard at Nuneaton on 29th July 1981. No. 6277 (YHA 277J), a Daimler Fleetline D13 with Alexander bodywork, carries the 'Hunter' fleetname and the horn logo now used on Nuneaton allocated buses. Two more vehicles, now over ten years old, stand beside the D13. They are Leyland Leopard S24, No. 6417 (CHA 417K), with a Willowbrook body and another Leopard, this time with Marshall bodywork, S26 No. 6470 (DHA 470K). By early 1981 the Midland Red double deck fleet was reduced to less than 100, representing only one ninth of the entire fleet. In 1964 the fleet contained almost 900 double deckers, a quantity greater than that of single deck service buses owned by Midland Red.
Rex Kennedy

Plate 134: Worcester, once a stronghold of Midland Red D12 double deckers which were used on the city services in the late 1960s, is now predominantly Leyland National territory. Apart from the Mk. 1 National which now operates services in the city, Worcester's allocation consists of only eight coaches, four dual-purpose Marshall bodied Leylands and one Leyland with a Willowbrook body. A far cry from days gone by when the variety in the Midland Red fleet was far greater than it is today. Operating the W32 city service route in Worcester, Midland Red Leyland National, No. 437 (GOL 437N), proceeds down Broad Street and is about to pass the bus station at Angel Place, on its way to its Bath Road destination.

Rex Kennedy

Plate 135: The livery of this Midland Red Leyland Leopard PSU3A, No. 6398 (YHA 398J), with Willowbrook bodywork, is somewhat surprising. It is a dual-purpose vehicle in the all-white coach livery and carrying National Express stickers, and is seen at Digbeth, Birmingham on 25th July 1981.

Andrew Kennedy

Plate 136: Midland Red B.M.M.O built S23, No. 5930 (RHA 930G), stands at Nuneaton garage on Saturday 28th February 1981. 'Final Day of B.M.M.O. Built Buses' — 1923-1981', is the information on the blind. Only three of these vehicles lasted until the end, Nos. 5930, 5937 and 5977. No. 5953 was to make her last run on Friday, 27th February 1981 and was the only one of the four to carry a local identity fleetname, 'Hunter', denoting allocation to Nuneaton garage. This picture was taken at Nuneaton whilst on an enthusiasts' special to Birmingham. Earlier in the day it had worked its last service from Leamington to Rugby.

Robert Powell Hendry

MIDLAND RED

Plate 132: Climbing towards the railway bridge south of Stafford, which crosses the main electrified railway line from Birmingham to Stafford and the north-west, a Leyland Leopard with Marshall bodywork, No. 334 (PHA 334M), a Midland Red type S28, works the 876 service to Wolverhampton on 27th November 1981. From 6th September 1981 Midland Red was split into five separate operating companies, Midland Red (South), (North), (East), (West) and (Express) Ltd. No. 334, pictured here, is in the Midland Red (North) company. The original Midland Red Omnibus Co. continues, but only to run Central Works at Carlyle Road, Birmingham.

Rex Kennedy

Plate 133: A Midland Red 1971 Leyland Leopard with Plaxton bodywork, No. 6453 (AHA 453J), swings round to enter Digbeth coach station on 25th July 1981. This vehicle is one of a batch of fifteen designated C12 of which only seven remain in the Midland Red fleet. Digbeth is the only garage of the new company Midland Red (Express) Ltd.

Andrew Kennedy

Plate 130: The town of Ashford is served by both East Kent and Maidstone & District vehicles. With the 710 service to Folkestone on 23rd November 1981, Maidstone & District VR, No. 5846 (BKE 846T), fitted with an ECW body, a lowbridge version with a height of 13 ft. 8 in., picks up more passengers before proceeding down the hill in the direction of the railway station. Maidstone & District is the only NBC subsidiary company to carry a large fleet number on the roof of the vehicle, as seen in this view. This practice of displaying fleet numbers on the front dome, facilitates the checking of bus movements, by overhead cameras, at Chatham bus station.

Rex Kennedy

Plate 131: A quantity of fast deteriorating withdrawn Maidstone & District vehicles lie on wasteland at the rear of Tenterden garage on 23rd November 1981. The three on view in this picture from left to right, are 1971 Leyland Leopard with a Willowbrook body, No. 3426 (AKM 426K), a 1964 Daimler Fleetline with Northern Counties bodywork, No. 6073 (73 YKT) and 1968 Leyland Leopard PSU3, No. 2804 (OKO 804G), fitted with Willowbrook body in dual-purpose livery. Prior to renumbering the Maidstone & District fleet in the 1960s, No. 6073 carried the fleet number LD73 indicating low-bridge double decker. More than fifteen of these vehicles were still in service at the end of 1981.

Rex Kennedy

HASTINGS & DISTRICT

Plate 128: The fine structure of the oval shaped Hawkhurst bus station, with its arrival and departure platforms and attractively designed roof, is situated adjacent to the garage. Maidstone & District buses which frequent this location carry the Hastings & District fleetname. On 23rd November 1981, after a day of unsettled weather, a 'Hastings' Leyland National, No. 3569 (VKE 569S) lies parked at the arrival platform prior to moving around to the opposite side of the bus station to take out a Tunbridge Wells service. Hawkhurst garage is now only a sub-garage to Silverhill.

Rex Kennedy

Plate 129: A Maidstone & District Leyland National, No. 3544 (KKL 544P), loads for Rye at Ashford on 23rd November 1981 beside the East Kent garage. Until 1973 this garage was under the ownership of Maidstone & District. The vehicle carries the Hastings & District fleetname, the only local identity name in the Maidstone & District fleet resulting from an M.A.P. survey in December 1980. The fleetname, in multi-coloured National style lettering, is on a vinyl sticker which has a green background covering the original Maidstone & District fleetname. The large dent on the front of the vehicle suggests an unfortunate bump at sometime or other.

Rex Kennedy

Plate 126: A Monday morning in the suburbs of Maidstone, as a Maidstone & District 1968 Leyland Leopard, No. 2816 (OKO 816G), with dual-purpose 49 seat body, picks up shoppers for Maidstone town. By the end of 1981 very few of these vehicles remained in the Maidstone & District fleet.
Rex Kennedy

Plate 127: Canterbury bus station lies within East Kent territory and can be found within the city walls. On 23rd November 1981, a 1974 Leyland National Mk. 1, of the Maidstone & District fleet, No. 3519 (RKE 519M), parks with Leyland Nationals of the East Kent fleet. This particular Mk. 1 National, together with Nos. 3514, 3516 and 3518 was on loan to East Kent at the time, but the sight of Maidstone & District buses, both double and single deck, arriving and departing on services covered by Maidstone & District is not uncommon at Canterbury bus station. Other vehicles on loan to East Kent from Maidstone & District in 1981, were open-topper No. 0620 (see **Plate 64**) and Nos. 4120, 4137 and 4140, Leyland Leopard Duple Dominants. East Kent also had vehicles on loan to Maidstone & District.
Andrew Kennedy

MAIDSTONE & DISTRICT

Plate 124: As a strong wind gets up at Tenterden on 23rd November 1981 and blows leaves across the main street, the Maidstone & District 919 service to London picks up from the quaint black and white half-timbered NBC travel office, surely a unique style of premises for the National Bus Company. Leyland Leopard, No. 2150 (BKJ 150T), with Duple bodywork, awaits departure with the 14.15 hrs. Tenterden to London (Victoria) service, arriving in London at 17.11 hrs. after passing through Maidstone, Swanley and Camberwell en route. The vehicle carries the dual-purpose green and white livery and the removable route board above the radiator. Some 919 services start from Maidstone but only two 919 services per day leave Tenterden.

Rex Kennedy

Plate 125: A new service, named 'Invictaway' was introduced, in October 1980, by Maidstone & District to operate between the Medway towns and Gatwick Airport. Three dual-purpose Leyland Leopard coaches have been repainted in all-black livery and all bear the name 'Invictaway' and a rearing horse logo on the front and sides. The vehicles chosen were No. 2147 (BKJ 147T), seen in this picture at Victoria coach station on 10th October 1981, the others being Nos. 2152 and 2153. A Leyland PDR1 double decker, No. 5179 (FKM 719L), with Metro-Cammell bodywork also carries a similar livery and has undergone a seating conversion changing the upper deck from 45 to 40 seats and the lower deck from 33 to 29 seats.

Andrew Kennedy

Plate 121: The 790 service which runs between Oxford and London (Victoria) is operated jointly by London Country (Greenline) and Oxford/South Midland. The Greenline coaches used, normally work off Amersham garage and MA51 seen on the side of the vehicle pictured here indicates this. The numbers MA51 and MA52, in fact, apply to two RB coaches which operate the 290 and 790 Oxford to London services. Greenline AEC Reliance, No. RB24 (TPD 24S), with Duple bodywork and sporting the fine green and white livery, is seen, on 14th July 1981, at Headington, about three miles from Oxford City Centre. The 790 service, en route to London, passes through High Wycombe, Uxbridge and Heathrow Airport and runs two hourly.

Andrew Kennedy

Plate 122: While southbound passengers study the timetable sheet at Dorking, London Country's Dorking allocated No. RP42 (JPA 142K) waits for a driver for Greenline route 714 to Kingston in May 1981. RP vehicles were phased out of Greenline working at Dorking during 1981, when the garage received new PL type coaches in the spring. The RP is an AEC Reliance with Park Royal bodywork fitted with special internal luggage racks. It replaced the RMC and RCL vehicle on Greenline coach services.

Ian Pringle

Plate 123: One could forgive the driver of 1972 AEC Reliance, No. RN3 (MRR 803K), fitted with 60 seat Plaxton bodywork, a quick look at the faresheet for London Country's once monthly service (854) from Guildford to Chichester. On Wednesday 3rd June 1981, a passenger boards at Alfold Cross Roads. This service only operates on the first Wednesday of every month and returns the same day. The vehicle was once owned by Barton of Nottingham where it carried the fleet number 1221, and it was acquired by London Country in 1977 together with others of similar design.

Ian Pringle

Plate 118: A stricken London Country Leyland Atlantean is rescued from its plight, as it seeks help from a breakdown vehicle in Hemel Hempstead in April 1981. The breakdown crew give the photographer a brief glance as they complete the recovery.
Kevin Lane

Plate 119: One of the more pleasant practices of London Country bus service routes is their habit of terminating at country inns, a most welcome facility for the flagging bus enthusiast on a hot summer afternoon. The Plough at Dormansland has appeared in timetables for many years, but sadly, with the demise of the East Grinstead garage at the end of 1981, the 485 service seen here, has been withdrawn. Leyland Atlantean, No. AN116 (MPJ 216L), a 1972 model with Metro-Cammell Weymann bodywork is pictured having worked this service in May 1981.
Ian Pringle

Plate 120: A typical London Country bus service scene, as 1972 Park Royal bodied Leyland Atlantean, No. AN26 (JPL 126K), pauses at Kemsing village Post Office, in Kent, in September 1981 on the local 467 service from Sevenoaks. Dunton Green garage received several AN vehicles in April 1981, which now operate on routes previously worked by single deckers. Note the new ultimate destination size Johnson type, on the via point blind.
Ian Pringle

Plate 116: A London Country 1977 Bristol LHS, No. BN60 (TPJ 60S), fitted with the narrow 7ft. 6in. body, braves the cold as it passes through the outskirts of St. Albans on 17th December 1981. It is working the 13.32 hrs. Borehamwood to Harpenden service. The vehicle is fitted with only 35 seats in comparison to the usual 43 seats of the normal standard LH design, and these vehicles are fast disappearing from the fleet.

Kevin Lane

Plate 117: The bright sunlight catches a London Country Leyland Atlantean PDR1, No. AN101 (MPJ 201L), as it runs into St. Albans with a 341 route working to Hatfield in the summer of 1981. This vehicle is fitted with the Metro-Cammell Weymann bodywork. London Country ordered the first 90 of these vehicles when introduced in 1972 but eventually took a total of 120, taking the remaining 30 built which were originally destined for Midland Red. Nos. AN1–90 were fitted with Park Royal bodies whilst Nos. AN91–120 had MCW bodywork.

Kevin Lane

Plate 114: Windsor in winter. With snow drifts against the castle walls, a London Country Leyland National Series 'B', No. SNB486 (BPL 486T), climbs the hill through the town on 13th December 1981. During summer months this area of the town is usually crowded with visitors.
Rex Kennedy

Plate 115: With a background of a disused railway bridge over one of the roads into Hemel Hempstead from a north-easterly direction, a London Country Leyland National Mk. 1, No. SNB80 (TPD 180M), swings round on to the main road from a local housing estate before proceeding into the town centre on 31st October 1981. In 1972 and early 1973 the NBC ordered 498 Leyland Nationals, with the order of 70 from London Country only being topped by that of the Northern General group with 75.
Rex Kennedy

NATIONAL WELSH
CYMRU CENEDLAETHOL

Plate 146: Emerging from beneath the railway bridge which carries the railway to Ebbw Vale Steelworks, National Welsh Leyland National Mk. 1, No. N2478 (WUH 166T), sporting the broad white band at the waist, proceeds up the valley towards Brynmawr on 24th November 1981. It is seen approaching the village of Cwm, with the entrance to Marine Colliery to the right of the picture. No. N2478 carries the fleetname 'Gwent Vales' where the NBC crest emblem is usually situated on the front of the vehicle.

Rex Kennedy

Plate 147: The bus station at Merthyr Tydfil lies adjacent to the new shopping precinct built in the 1970s. The orange and white vehicles of Merthyr Tydfil Borough Transport outnumber those of National Welsh at this location. On 23rd July 1981, an ex-Red & White National Welsh dual-purpose Leyland National, No. ND4175 (KDW 349P), lies parked in the open area of the bus station, and like all National Welsh buses, carries the Welsh equivalent, 'Cymru Cenedlaethol' on the offside of the vehicle, the name 'National Welsh' being carried on the nearside.

Andrew Kennedy

Plate 148: On 23rd July 1981 two National Welsh unlicenced Bristol RESL6L vehicles with ECW bodywork, ex-Red & White, lay in the yard at the rear of Aberdare garage. The withdrawn vehicle in this view, Regn. No. LAX 104E, with destination blind removed, last carried the fleet number RS3267 and, in 1972 whilst in the Red & White fleet was numbered RS467. The picture shows the NBC crest on the radiator but the National Welsh name has been obliterated from the vehicle. RESL indicates the shorter 33 ft. version of the RE with only 46 seats. This vehicle had a short reprieve in April 1981 when it was brought back into service after previously being withdrawn late in 1980.

Rex Kennedy

Plate 151: A National Welsh Leyland National, No. N3276 (NWO 477R), heads for Abergavenny as it passes through the streets of Hereford on 10th August 1981. Generally speaking, only Bristol REs and Leyland Nationals work into Hereford on National Welsh services, but the old Red & White Motor Services garage at Hereford closed nearly eleven years ago. 'Gwent Vales' is the area identity name carried below the windscreen of the vehicle. All Saints Church, built in the early thirteenth century, can be seen at the end of the street.

Andrew Kennedy

Plate 149: The once cream and blue buses of Jones of Aberbeeg were acquired by the National Bus Company in April 1969, and placed under the management of Red & White Motor Services. From 1973 the fleet was painted blue and white and displayed the double 'N' National bus symbol. When Jones of Aberbeeg, together with Red & White and Western Welsh were reformed as National Welsh in April 1978, Jones still retained the blue livery until 1979. This picture shows Jones' garage at Aberbeeg up for sale on 23rd July 1981, as a National Welsh 1971 Bristol RELH with Plaxton coachwork, No. RC7171 (XWO 939J), in NBC white coach livery reverses into the garage. The fleetname 'Jones Aberbeeg' is in blue lettering. Since 26th October 1980 this garage was only used as a coach depot and was eventually closed in November 1981.

Andrew Kennedy

Plate 150: Eight Leyland 'Redline' 440EA Asco Minibuses were in the National Welsh fleet. On 23rd July 1981, three of these vehicles were to be seen on Cwmbran garage. These minibuses are fitted with 19 high backed seats and the National Welsh name is carried in a white oval panel in front of the sliding door. No. MD1478 (WUH 178T) lay parked in the yard adjacent to the garage. Six of the original eight minibuses, excluding the one on view, had been withdrawn by the end of 1981.

Rex Kennedy

Plate 152: Pending inspection in the maintenance workshop at the National Welsh garage at Aberdare on 23rd July 1981, is a National Welsh Leyland National, No. 2775 (KDW 339P), raised upon the hydraulic ramp. An appropriate advert enhances the side of this vehicle. This garage has one of the largest allocations in the National Welsh fleet, the largest being at Porth, the old Rhondda garage. 'Cynon-Dare' is the local name given to buses in this area, a name in use since May 1980. Close by, in the same open area as the National Welsh garage, stands the Cynon Valley Borough Council garage, complete with buses and cleansing department vehicles, once going under the name of Aberdare Urban District Council.

Rex Kennedy

Plate 153: The mobile wash at Aberdare ex-Red & White National Welsh garage passes along a National Welsh un-manned ECW bodied Bristol RELH, No. RD5371 (XWO 172J), on 23rd July 1981. The vehicle is in dual-purpose livery with high backed seats and is ex-Red & White Motor Services. This type of washing plant passes on rails along each side of the bus enabling the vehicle to remain stationary whilst washing is carried out.

Rex Kennedy

Plate 155: The famous Monnow Gate at Monmouth makes a picturesque setting as a 10.3 metre Leyland National, No. NS1479 (YBO 147T), of the National Welsh fleet, negotiates the archway as it crosses the River Monnow on 24th November 1981. This Norman fortification is the remaining one of four gates into Monmouth, consisting of a portcullis, eyelets for archers, and holes through which boiling water or molten lead could be poured upon the enemy, and was built in 1270. It would be sad to see locations such as this disappear in Britain, as has the opportunity to photograph buses passing beneath Beverley Bar in Yorkshire.

Rex Kennedy

Plate 154: The bus station at Monmouth which is situated beside the National Welsh garage is surrounded by tall trees. On 25th August 1981, No. HR5567 (JKG 489F), a Daimler Fleetline with Metro-Cammell bodywork, stood off duty in the sunshine beside a National Welsh Bristol RELH No. RC6971 (XWO 937J), with a 51 seat Plaxton body, minus its radiator grille. No. HR5567 is ex-City of Cardiff Transport vehicle No. 489, and has unusually designed front and upper windows and was one of about nine Fleetlines purchased by National Welsh from City of Cardiff in 1979.

Rex Kennedy

Plate 156: Two small bus stations exist at Neath, one at the railway station and the other at Victoria Gardens. The station location is used predominantly by South Wales Transport buses, whereas Victoria Gardens, pictured here on 24th November 1981, is used by National Welsh, South Wales Transport and Cream Line Services (Tonmawr) Ltd., an independent which adds a splash of colour to the area. Preparing to load for Bridgend, a dual-purpose Leyland National, No. ND4775 (KDW 355P), of the National Welsh fleet, stands at this quite photogenic location as the driver takes the fares. On this occasion, the queue was rather long, making the operation of fare taking an arduous task in these days of one man operation. 'Glan-Ogwr' displayed on the front of the vehicle is the name introduced during 1980 for vehicles in the Bridgend area.
Andrew Kennedy

Plate 157: The Forest of Dean in Gloucestershire is one of the few areas in England where National Welsh provide a service. Their garage at Cinderford is located in the heart of this beautiful part of England and services from here and Monmouth run into Gloucester, Ross-on-Wye and Chepstow. On 24th November 1981, National Welsh Leyland Leopard, No. U872 (XBO 538K), with Marshall bodywork climbs up the hill in the direction of Gloucester soon after making a detour into the village of Longhope seen in the distance. This route to Gloucester covers undulating country giving exciting views towards the Severn estuary. Also on view is one of the few double deckers owned by the local independent operator, Cottrell's of Micheldean working a local service.

Rex Kennedy

Plate 158: An interesting trio of National Welsh double deckers could be seen, on 23rd July 1981, at Cwmbran garage. Each of these vehicles generates interest. To the left, No. LR5669 (PKG 367H), withdrawn in October 1981, is ex-South Wales Transport No. 901 in 1979, and prior to that was in the Western Welsh fleet from new as No. 367, being sold to South Wales in 1972. The numbering system indicates the vehicle was built in 1969, the last two digits of the fleet number giving this information. The first two digits provide the actual number of the vehicle, No. LR5669 is a Northern Counties bodied Leyland PDR1. In the centre stands a Bristol VR, No. LR8051 (GTX 748W), new in October 1980, providing the new style of fleet number now indicating the year of delivery in the first two digits. On the far right of the picture is another 1969 vehicle of similar design to No. LR5669. This Leyland PDR1, with Northern Counties bodywork, No. LR2769 (PKG 373H), also originally in the Western Welsh fleet, never passed to South Wales Transport before inclusion in the National Welsh fleet. All these vehicles now carry the 'Gwent Vales' local identity name.

Rex Kennedy

Plate 159: Two National Welsh training vehicles stand in Tredegar garage on 23rd July 1981. The double decker, No. T1 (20 AAX), is a Bristol FL6G with ECW bodywork, originally fitted with 70 seats and once carrying the fleet No. L2060 for Red & White Motor Services, indicating its year of manufacture as 1960. Red & White were the largest customer for the Bristol FL double decker, taking twenty in all, and No. L1060 (10 AAX) remained in service until 1980. Only 45 Bristol FLs were produced and were a 30ft. version of the FS. These vehicles were never very popular and production only lasted for four years from 1960-1963. Beside the FL stands a 1962 Leyland Leopard with a 45 seat Willowbrook body. This vehicle, (605 BBO), was once numbered 605 in the Western Welsh fleet and on joining National Welsh was renumbered U5262. It now carries the number T3.

Rex Kennedy

Plate 160: During rush periods at Cheltenham St. Margaret's Road coach station, the approach roads are littered with cars picking up and dropping off friends and relatives at this busy location. The coach drivers encounter a formidable task as they weave their vehicles towards the ex-Black & White coach station. On 24th August 1981, National Welsh 1970 Plaxton bodied Leyland Leopard, No. UD370 (SKG 180H), nears its destination. On relegation to semi-coach duties, this vehicle was renumbered UD370 from UC370. It now carries the 'Gwent Vales' sticker on the side.

Rex Kennedy

Plate 161: On 7th February 1981, a line up of various designs of National Welsh vehicles was seen at Bulwark, Chepstow. Included were the two vehicles seen here, No. U1172 (XBO 541K), a 1972 ex-Western Welsh Leyland PSU3B with Marshall bodywork and No. RD5169 (SAX 7G), a 1969 Bristol RELL6G with an ECW body in dual-purpose livery, an ex-Red & White Motor Services Ltd. vehicle. Bulwark, Chepstow was once the head office and main works for Red & White, but now the National Welsh head office is situated in Cardiff, the original registered office of Western Welsh.

Rex Kennedy

Plate 162: Ex-Red & White 1971 Bristol RELL, No. R3971 (BWO 101K), now in the National Welsh fleet, passes the terraced cottages of Blaina with a school bus from Brynmawr on 24th November 1981. It is travelling in the direction of Abertillery, and on the front carries the 'Cynon-Dare' symbol familiar to the Aberdare area, the name being derived from the two rivers in that area.

Rex Kennedy

Plate 163: Approaching the large bus station at Newport, Gwent on 23rd July 1981, a Bristol VR, delivered to National Welsh in September 1980, No. LR8044 (GTX 741W), negotiates the narrow streets before confronting the hive of bus activity usually found at Newport bus station. National Welsh share the bus station at Newport with the Borough of Newport Transport who are noted for their Metro-Cammell Scania vehicles. A Newport Transport dual-doored single decker of this design follows the National Welsh VR. 'Gwent Vales' again appears on the front of this vehicle, a local identity name which was introduced in the Gwent and Rhymney Valley areas on 26th October 1980.

Rex Kennedy

NORTHERN

Plate 164: Northern General were the first NBC subsidiary which have managed to generally deviate from the standard red and green corporate liveries. Although some vehicles remain painted red in this fleet, many are in yellow, adding yet more of this colour to the area already dominated by the yellow and white of the Tyne & Wear Metro and PTE buses. In September 1981, a Northern Leyland Atlantean, No. 3482 (AUP 382W), with Roe bodywork, climbs up through the town of South Shields on a Newcastle service. The vehicles painted in a variation of the PTE's yellow livery are for use on local services within the PTE area, and the fleetname on the front of the vehicle is in red.

Kevin Lane

Plate 165: 1980 saw the introduction of the Metrobus to the Northern General fleet. The original batch was numbered 3486 to 3500 and No. 3486 (DVK 486W), is pictured here climbing into Gateshead in March 1981, leaving behind the mass of steel girders which make up the many rail and road bridges which lie in the vicinity of the original River Tyne separating Gateshead from Newcastle. These 76 seat MCW Metrobuses with Metro-Cammell bodies were first introduced in 1977, the first production models appearing in January 1978. The first operators to take delivery of these very reliable vehicles were London Transport and West Midlands PTE. The National Bus Company ordered their first Metrobuses in 1980, with deliveries going to Northern General, Maidstone & District and Bristol Omnibus Co. These vehicles now also appear throughout the municipal and PTE networks in Britain. In the first four years of production, the Metrobus has achieved great success and is firmly established as one of the most successful new double deckers in Britain and together with the new Leyland Olympian, sets a new trend in design as we see the Fleetlines, Atlanteans and VRs being phased out.

Geoff Coxon

Plate 166: The large Northern garage at Chester-le-Street is clearly visible from the A1 (M) road which travels from Scotch Corner to Newcastle upon Tyne. On 30th August 1981, two 1971 dual-doored Daimler Fleetline single deckers, with Alexander bodywork, in the red Northern livery, line up under the company name at the back of the depot, which is visible from the motorway. No. 4188 (KCN 10J), now withdrawn, is sporting the white band below the windows and carries the Alexander 'W' type body introduced in 1964 to accommodate a higher proportion of standing passengers. Originally fitted to a Leyland Panther chassis the 'W' type body was tried on a Daimler Fleetline chassis in 1969, resulting in orders from NBC subsidiaries such as Northern, Yorkshire Traction and Potteries Motor Traction.

Rex Kennedy

Plate 168: Newcastle upon Tyne town centre sees a combination of NBC's Northern and United fleets on service, in addition to the Tyne & Wear PTE buses prolific in the area. On 19th June 1981, a Park Royal bodied Leyland Atlantean, No. 3286 (RCN 112N), of the Northern NBC fleet, rounds a traffic island at the north end of the city and carries the yellow 'Tyne & Wear' livery with the broad white band. Since this picture was taken, this vehicle has been converted from a dual-doored version to single door only. This vehicle, prior to 1976, was in the Gateshead & District fleet.

Rex Kennedy

Plate 169: The unusual sight of an all-red coach in the NBC fleet is seen inside Chester-le-Street garage on 30th August 1981. This 1972 Northern Bristol RE coach, with an ECW body, No. 5035 (MCN 884L), has since been renumbered 4884 and its livery creates a pleasant change from the standard NBC coach liveries. The Northern garage at Chester-le-Street provides a variety of bus designs, housing both double and single deckers and beside the RE coach stands a conventional Leyland National Mk. 1, No. 4616 (APT 616S). Chester-le-Street garage is one of the larger garages in the Northern network with an allocation only smaller than that of Philadelphia.

Rex Kennedy

◁ **Plate 167:** South of the River Tyne in Gateshead in September 1981, a 1972 ex-Gateshead & District dual-doored Leyland Atlantean PDR1, No. 3229 (NCN 105L), with ECW bodywork, now in the Northern fleet, stops to set down passengers on a local service. It carries the Tyne & Wear PTE yellow livery. Since the total re-organisation of bus services in the Newcastle upon Tyne area in November 1981, the only 'yellow' Northern service to cross the Tyne Bridge is service 301, with many Northern services terminating at Gateshead and Heworth Metro stations.

Kevin Lane

Plate 170: An all-yellow 1972 Northern, a Daimler Fleetline with Willowbrook body, No. 4240 (LCN 506K), crosses the traffic lights in Newcastle upon Tyne on 19th June 1981. This vehicle is an ex-Tynemouth & District bus acquired by Northern in 1975 on the takeover of the entire Tynemouth & District fleet within the NBC network. From the year 1969, Tynemouth & District were a separate NBC subsidiary and this vehicle (ex-Tynemouth No. 2806), is ironically, on this occasion, seen on service for Tynemouth. Since November 1981, Northern have relinquished service 306 (Newcastle to Tynemouth) giving United full operation.

Rex Kennedy

Plate 171: Lowestoft, the home of Eastern Coachworks, sees buses painted in the liveries of many different companies as they are out-shopped from the works. In November 1981, a new Northern Leyland Olympian, No. 3593 (JTY 393X), stands awaiting delivery to the north east where it will receive its destination blinds. In the background is a new Trans-Clyde Olympian awaiting delivery to Glasgow. The Leyland Olympian was introduced in 1981 to replace the, now out of production, Fleetline, the Bristol VRT and eventually the Atlantean.

Dave Savage

Plate 172: A Northern Willowbrook bodied Leyland coach, No. 5086 (TUP 586V), is pictured at Durham bus station on 26th July 1981. In dual-purpose local coach livery, she stands overlooked by the fine railway viaduct which carries the main line from Darlington to Newcastle upon Tyne. The bus station is used jointly with United and National Express services in conjunction with various independent operators.

Dave Savage

OXFORD SOUTH MIDLAND

Plate 173: In 1981, City of Oxford Motor Services now operating under the fleetname Oxford/South Midland, celebrated 100 years of public transport. To commemorate this event a Bristol VR, No. 476 (HUD 476S), was painted in the old City of Oxford pre-NBC livery, and this vehicle is seen here at Cowley Road garage, Oxford, on 25th May 1981, the day the vehicle was officially released from the workshops after repainting. No. 476 is fitted with a trans-dot destination display, and whilst in service the locations covered en route reappear in the panel at short intervals. The Centenary event was also celebrated by an 'Open Day' at Cowley Road garage, Oxford, on 12th September. This event created tremendous interest and proved to be an excellent public relations exercise. Vehicles on display covered a period of manufacture from 1915 to 1981. Another Bristol VR, in the old City of Oxford livery, No. 454 (YBW 601R), was painted in 1981 and in this particular case the vehicle carried the pre-war livery of maroon and duck egg green with a white roof.

Andrew Kennedy

Plate 174: Eight serviceable ex-London Transport DMS Daimler double deckers with bodywork by Metro-Cammell have been bought by Oxford/South Midland. On Saturday, 25th July 1981, No. 994 (JGU 275K), ex-London Transport No. DMS1275, one of five now painted in the Park & Ride livery of red, white and blue with a grey skirt, slowly proceeds along Cornmarket Street, Oxford, towards the outskirts of the city where large car-parks are situated. The 'Park & Ride' scheme was introduced in an effort to avoid congestion of heavy traffic in the city centre and incorporates three routes with parking on the south, north and west of town, the three car-parks having provision for 1,500 cars in all.

Rex Kennedy

Plate 175: Passing through the one way system in Aylesbury town centre, Oxford/South Midland Bristol VRT, No. 497 (HUD 497W), starts its journey back to Oxford via Thame on the 280 service on Sunday, 1st November 1981. This vehicle was delivered to Oxford/South Midland in August 1980, being one of twenty-one VRTs bought in that year. Almost 100 of these vehicles now operate in the Oxford/South Midland fleet. Aylesbury garage is operated jointly by United Counties and Oxford/South Midland and is the only garage of this fleet outside the Oxfordshire boundary.

Andrew Kennedy

Plate 176: No. 388 (MJO 388 an Oxford/South Midland 19 Daimler Fleetline, with North Counties bodywork, negotiates newly laid cobbles at the end of pedestrian area in Queen Str Oxford, on Saturday, 25th J 1981. These vehicles are now the course of gradual withdra from the fleet. The additio mouldings beneath the windo show the boundaries of the du egg green livery once carried this vehicle. The paved areas the City of Oxford, altho generally traffic free, are used buses and taxis, and in these ar queue conductors operate tak fares at the bus queues, prior the arrival of the bus, ther speeding up one man operat now in force.

Rex Kenne

Plate 177: The attractive design of the Alexander bodied Daimler Fleetline is clearly visible in this view. Oxford/South Midland No. 398 (TFC 398K), a 1971 version, slowly moves towards the city centre in Oxford on 25th July 1981 on a cross town service. The 'Fleetline' was designed in response to the 'Atlantean' and its dropped centre axle permitted low height bodies. Production of this model has now ceased in favour of the Titan and Olympian.

Rex Kennedy

Plate 178: The toll bridge at Swinford, on the outskirts of Eynsham, traverses the River Thames near Pinkhill Lock on the Oxford to Fulbrook, Oxford/South Midland route. Service buses are exempt from 'on the spot' tolls when crossing this bridge. On 12th November 1981, Oxford/South Midland, No. 108 (NUD 108L), a Bristol VRT with an ECW body, slowly leaves the bridge to continue its journey. This particular vehicle was one of nine bought in 1973 and fitted with coach seating for use on weekend London services. At that time they were painted with the top half completely white and the lower half in red, and had a top speed of 65 m.p.h. Since being demoted to general services, all except No. 101 have been repainted in the red livery shown in this picture. No. 101 is also destined for a repaint.

Rex Kennedy

Plate 179: The Oxford to London 190 shuttle service is now half-hourly and hourly from Carterton to London. This 'Pay As You Enter' service is so popular that extra coaches are often run and provision has now been made to operate a 15 minute service in 1982. The special livery of red, orange, blue and white certainly draws attention to the Leyland Leopards of the Oxford/South Midland fleet Nos. 1–27 and 49–51. On 4th January 1981, No. 6 (LWL 6S), sporting this livery, prepares to depart for London (Victoria) with the 11.50 hrs. Sunday service. Standing behind is Leyland Leopard No. 19 (YFC 19V), with a 790 service, (**see Plate 121**), which passes through High Wycombe en route for Heathrow Airport. Leyland Leopard No. 19 is one of six, (19–24), delivered to Oxford/South Midland in 1979 replacing the cancelled order for dual-purpose Leyland Nationals with high speed axles for use on the fast London services, leaving Oxford/South Midland as the only NBC subsidiary not operating Leyland Nationals within their bus service fleet. The 190 fast service claims to reach its destination, from Oxford, in 100 minutes and is only £2.97 return.

Rex Kennedy

CARTERTON-OXFORD-LONDON

Plate 180: The London (Victoria) terminus for the 190 Oxford/South Midland service lies just inside the entrance to the coach station. Ex-Potteries Motor Traction Leyland Leopard, with Duple coachwork, now Oxford/South Midland No. 50 (URF 50S), stands empty after arrival from Oxford on 10th October 1981. In the background another arrival on this service approaches worked by No. 15 (WUD 815T). Two designs of Duple Dominant coachwork can be seen, with No. 50 carrying Mk. 2 Option 1 bodywork, and No. 15 carrying the Mk. 2 Option 2 style with the deeper windscreen. Nos. 49–51 in the Oxford/South Midland fleet were on loan for a month from PMT before being purchased in May 1981, and these three vehicles carried the same fleet numbers whilst in the PMT fleet.

Andrew Kennedy

Plate 182: After negotiati the narrow 'two-way' g between the Sun Inn and o dwellings in the Oxfordsh village of Wheatley, Oxfo South Midland Ford R10 No. 667 (WWL 504R), w Duple Dominant bus boc work, climbs away up incline on 31st Decemb 1981. The 230 serv meanders through ma country lanes on its ro from Oxford to Thar visiting seven Oxfordshire a Buckinghamshire villa during the course of journey.

Rex Kenne

Ford Duples on service

Plate 181: In 1976 Oxford/South Midland initially purchased eight Ford R1014 single deckers fitted with 43 seats and having Duple Dominant service bus bodywork. These were numbered 666–673, but No. 666 caught fire whilst on service at Chinnor in 1979 and was withdrawn. The remaining seven are allocated to Oxford, Witney, Chipping Norton and Wantage garages. On 31st October 1981, No. 671 (WWL 508R) returns to Witney and is seen leaving Faringdon after connecting with the Bristol Omnibus service to Swindon. These vehicles were introduced mainly for country services and only 50 with this particular bodywork were built for the National Bus Company in 1976, the largest user being South Wales Transport with seventeen.

Rex Kennedy

Plate 183: No doubt one of the smallest NBC garages in Britain. Great Milton still proudly displays the old City of Oxford company name, and is situated only nine miles from Oxford. It now houses only one vehicle, as the vehicle length precludes the sliding doors being moved to allow entry for a second vehicle. Surrounded by snow on 13th December 1981, Oxford/South Midland Bristol RELL, No. 679 (JEH 179K), with ECW bodywork, protrudes from the garage entrance. This 1972 vehicle was acquired from Potteries Motor Traction in the summer of 1981 along with two similar single deckers, Nos. 676 and 678. These REs carried the fleet numbers 176, 178 and 179 whilst in PMT ownership.

Andrew Kennedy

Plate 184: Dual purpose 1973 Bristol RELH, No. 77 (NUD 77M), of the Oxford/South Midland fleet, climbs the hill towards Headington with a 230 Oxford service from Thame. These vehicles are sometimes used on the fast 190 route to London on busy days and weekends, as comfortable coach type seating is fitted.

Rex Kennedy

Plate 185: A shortened version of ex-Midland Red 1971 Ford R192, with Plaxton bodywork, now in the Oxford/South Midland fleet, and fitted with 27 seats. Carrying the fleet No. 674 (YHA 393J), it is seen alongside Wantage garage in January 1981 prior to withdrawal in July. The conversion from 45 to 27 seats was carried out by Midland Red and it was acquired by Oxford/South Midland in 1978. The numbering policy of Oxford/South Midland is to prefix all fleet numbers of single deck service buses with a figure 6.

Andrew Kennedy

POTTERIES

Plate 186: High pressure cleaning at Hanley garage as PMT Bristol VR, No. 695 (GRF 695V), sits high on the hydraulic ramp on 27th November 1981. In the same area, situated behind the garage, is the wash bay. The entire double deck fleet of PMT consists of Bristol VRTs with the exception of a single Dennis Dominator and the Foden Northern Counties, having now lost their Leyland PDR1s with Weymann bodies and Alexander bodied Daimler Fleetlines.

Rex Kennedy

Plate 187: Standing parked outside the Queens Theatre, Burslem, a PMT Bristol RELL, No. 226 (PVT 226L), rests before carrying out its next duty on 27th November 1981. At this time, the entire PMT fleet consisted of about 235 vehicles, of which 32 were Bristol REs. This particular vehicle carries the words 'Colliery Bus' on its destination blind, a common sight in this part of the country.

Andrew Kennedy

Plate 188: A view of the yard looking from the inside of Hanley PMT garage. Hanley shares with Newcastle-under-Lyme the distinction of being one of the largest garages in the PMT network, and was opened in February 1953. On 27th November 1981, three Duple bodied Leyland Leopard coaches, two in dual-purpose livery, stand parked with a 'National Express' white liveried coach. From right to left the Potteries coaches are Nos. 48 (SEH 275N), 56 (XBF 56S) and 66 (GRF 266V). The centre coach carries the 'Intatown' name above the radiator. 'Intatown' is a fast 'limited stop' service operated between Hanley and Crewe using the A500 trunk road. Two vehicles in the PMT fleet carry the name 'Intatown', No. 56 pictured here and No. 57 (XBF 57S). No. 56 has since been painted in a 'special' livery. Beside these three coaches stands a PMT 1978 Bristol VRT, No. 672 (URF 672S), with 13 ft. 5 in. extra low ECW bodywork.

Rex Kennedy

Plate 189: On 27th November 1981, a Potteries Bristol VRT, No. 632 (KRE 632P), passes beneath the bridges which carry the main electrified railway line to the north-west and are situated at the north end of Stoke-on-Trent station. The bridge shows a 13 ft. 9 in. clearance and this particular vehicle has a height of 13 ft. 5 in. and was introduced by ECW in 1973, being 3 in. lower than the standard lowbridge design. The lower version is instantly recognisable by the lack of a white band above the windscreen. The new lower height was welcomed by Maidstone & District, Yorkshire Traction, United Counties and Oxford/South Midland in addition to PMT.

Rex Kennedy

P.M.T. Oddities

Plate 190: Potteries Motor Traction has in its fleet a solitary Dennis Dominator double decker, No. 700 (XBF 700S), a 74 seater with Alexander 'D' type body work. The Dennis leaf suspension is reputed to give an extremely smooth ride. A similar vehicle was delivered to Central SMT. The National Bus Company has only six 'Dominators' in their entire fleet. Five Willowbrook normal height versions are with Maidstone & District and the only Alexander bodied low height model is with PMT, and is seen on this occasion at Newcastle under Lyme bus station on 27th November 1981.

Rex Kennedy

Plate 191: Another vehicle with PMT having the distinction of being the only one of its kind in the Potteries fleet is a Leyland 47 seater coach with Willowbrook body, No. 22 (OEH 22W). Delivered new in June 1981, and fitted with tinted windows, this coach is seen awaiting departure from Digbeth coach station, Birmingham on 25th July 1981 with a London service, only a matter of weeks after delivery to PMT. It is noticeable that certain vehicles in this fleet, like the coach in this picture, carry the name 'Potteries' which is gradually replacing the old PMT fleetname.

Andrew Kennedy

Plate 192: The last of the three 'oddities' in the PMT fleet is the Foden 74 seat double decker, No. 900 (WVT 900S), fitted with Northern Counties bodywork. The unusual design of this vehicle is clearly seen in this view taken, whilst on service, at Newcastle under Lyme in November 1981. Both the 'Foden' and 'Dennis' seen in **Plate 190** are allocated to Newcastle garage. Northern Counties double deck bodies have been fitted in the past to PMT vehicles, but only to Daimler Fleetline chassis.

Dave Savage

Plate 193: Captured by the winter sunshine whilst on service near Hanley, Stoke-on-Trent, PMT Leyland National Mk. 1, No. 283 (KRE 283P), slows down to pick up passengers before continuing its journey to Stafford. This vehicle pictured on 27th November 1981, still displays the 'Prince of Wales' plume of feathers below the windscreen and the 'Royal Wedding' celebration sticker on the side, four months after the event.
Rex Kennedy

Plate 194: The entire area of Stoke-on-Trent, Hanley, Fenton, Longton, Burslem and Newcastle under Lyme in the Potteries, is a vast built up conurbation, and one has difficulty in distinguishing the boundaries between these towns. Heading from the direction of Hanley town centre on 27th November 1981, a PMT Bristol RELL No. 229 (PVT 229L) proceeds towards one of the other 'Potteries' towns. The vehicle was in the last batch of REs delivered to Potteries Motor Traction in 1972/73.
Andrew Kennedy

Plate 195: Passing one of the older buildings, with a unique engraving built into the Tudor style upper storey, in Hanley, Stoke-on-Trent, a PMT Leyland National, No. 243 (PVT 243L), heads down the hill en route for Wedgwoods, famous for its china. This vehicle previously carried a white band painted below its windows, but is now in the all-red livery as a result of NBC revisions, which excluded the white bands on repainting single deck vehicles.
Rex Kennedy

Plate 199: One of (PTF 764L) and i the seating capacit National Bus Com underlined. All we and dual-purpose v

Plate 196: With the vast panorama of the Potteries area in the distance, an 11.3 metre Leyland National of the PMT fleet, No. 232 (PVT 232L), makes the long climb into Burslem town centre before continuing its journey, service 310, to Hanley on 27th November 1981. At the foot of the hill seen in this view, lies the Burslem PMT garage having an allocation of just under 50 vehicles. The garage, in Scotia Road, was originally constructed in 1929 having since been extensively rebuilt.
Rex Kennedy

Plate 200: One of the n panies that loaned vehicle Yorkshire PTE to o Sheffield was Ribble. Du Sheffield was an location for the bus enabling him to see a vehicle designs and ope March 1981, Ribble lo 1316 (RTF 627M), a Atlantean with a Park R and No. 1480 (TRN 480V Atlantean with ECW bod South Yorkshire PTE. Or 1981, No. 1480 was seen in Sheffield but at that ti carry the South Yorks number in addition to t number, whereas vehicl from other operators carrying two numbers.
Adr

Coach Liveries

Plate 201: A regular motorway express service, X43, is operated by Ribble between Manchester and Burnley. This 'Timesaver' service, as portrayed on the front of Leyland Leopard, No. 1121 (WCK 121V), with Duple Dominant coachwork, is operated by special liveried coaches, and on 31st December 1981, this vehicle was seen wending its way through the heavily congested area of Manchester Piccadilly which is normally packed solid with Greater Manchester PTE vehicles. No. 1121 was painted in the special X43 livery in November 1981 after No. 1123 was outshopped in a similar livery during October 1981. The X43 route was once operated by Ribble double deck coaches.
Peter W. Robinson

Plate 202: Burnley, situated in what was the centre of the cotton weaving industry, sees both Ribble services and local Burnley & Pendle Joint Transport Committee operations. The Ribble garage, seen in the background in this view, has an allocation of approximately 40 vehicles, and National Travel (West) coaches can also be found at this location. With a service for Manchester on 14th November 1981, Ribble dual-purpose liveried Leyland Leopard, No. 1089 (YFR 489R), fitted with a Duple body, leaves Burnley to head south.
Andrew Kennedy

Plate 203: A Ribble vehicle having had an interesting life over recent years is a 1969 Plaxton bodied Leyland Leopard coach No. 964 (HRN 964G). Late in 1978 this vehicle was de-licenced for disposal and in January 1979, was hired to West Yorkshire together with Ribble coaches Nos. 957, 958, 962 and 975 of similar design. However, in June 1981, No. 964 was hired to National Travel (West) with Nos. 958, 962 and 975 and was to be seen at Cheltenham coach station on 13th August 1981 having worked a Liverpool to Cheltenham service. On 31st October 1981 this vehicle was placed in the National Travel (West) disposal pool.
Dave Savage

Series 'B' Nationals

Plate 204: A Ribble Series 'B' Leyland National climbs out of Kendal town centre with a local service in December 1981. No. 804 (TRN 804V), pictured here, was delivered new to Ribble in July 1979 and was one of eleven in the batch delivered, following the prototype No. 801 (GCW 461S), of the new 44 seat 'Economy' version of the Leyland National. This was the only batch of Series 'B' Nationals purchased by Ribble who quickly followed this with orders for Mk. 2 versions.
Peter W. Robinson

Plate 205: The Series 'B' Leyland National is recognisable at the front by the three sets of vents beneath the windscreen. No. 812 (TRN 812V), of the Ribble fleet, awaits departure from Nelson bus station on 14th November 1981, a location also used by the local Burnley & Pendle cream and maroon buses. The districts of Colne and Nelson were combined in a local government re-shuffle on 1st April 1974 to form the new borough of Pendle. The Pendle District is renowned for the infamous legendary 'Lancashire Witch', hence this logo appears on some of the Burnley & Pendle vehicles.
Andrew Kennedy

SOUTHDOWN

Plate 206: Hants & Dorset together with Southampton Transport jointly operate the local Southampton route 54 which passes through Northam, the scene of this picture, en route from West End to Southampton railway station. In June 1981, a Southdown vehicle was photographed on this service which was a most unusual occurrence. Bristol VR, No. 584 (SNJ 684R), owned by Southdown, was on loan to Hants & Dorset, at the time, in an exchange deal with Hants & Dorset who in turn reciprocated by handing over one of their Bristol VRs, No. 3369 (RPR 715R), for use by Southdown.

Kevin Lane

Coach Liveries

Plate 208: Flightline 777 is a non-stop service introduced in May 1981 between London (Victoria), Gatwick Airport and Crawley bus station. The route is operated jointly between London Country (Greenline) and Southdown. A Plaxton bodied Leyland Leopard of the Southdown fleet, No. 1341 (MAP 341W), stands in its allocated bay at Victoria coach station in December 1981, and is one of two painted in the special '777' livery, together with No. 1340. The livery is white, green and gold, and Nos. 1340 and 1341 were new to the Southdown fleet in March 1981. Nos. 1340 to 1353 were all originally ordered with Willowbrook bodies, but prior to delivery the order was cancelled and they were bodied by Plaxton.
Andrew Kennedy

Plate 209: Proudly carrying the traditional Southdown apple green livery and scroll fleet-name, No. 1822 (UUF 322J), a 1971 Leyland Leopard coach with Plaxton Panorama Elite II bodywork, stands parked in Battersea Gardens, London on 24th October 1981. Southdown have operated twenty five coaches of this design, six now painted in this original livery. These are Nos. 1822, 1828, 1831, 1833, 1835 and 1836.
Geoff Mills

Plate 207: Opposite the garage seen in **Plate 210**, the larger Southdown bus garage of the two at Hilsea, near Portsmouth, proudly displays the company name together with its National Bus Company association. This white painted building is a fine advertisement for the Southdown company. After picking up passengers, a Southdown Leyland Atlantean, No. 703 (PUF 133M), with Park Royal bodywork and fitted with white window rubbers, pulls away and heads towards the coast at Southsea on 7th November 1981. In 1974/75, Southdown purchased 47 Leyland Atlanteans of which 41 were bodied by Park Royal out of a total of 174 built by them in the series, although some of the others were dual-doored. The remaining six were fitted with Roe bodies. The majority of these Atlanteans are based at the garage pictured here. A number of others are based at Brighton.
Rex Kennedy

Plate 210: Hilsea Southdown garage, near Portsmouth, consists of two separate buildings, one on either side of the main dual carriageway linking the main A27 east/west trunk road with Portsmouth. On 7th November 1981, inside the building on the west side of the road, a Southdown Leyland Leopard coach, No. 1267 (LWV 267P), was to be seen. This design differs considerably from the 'Panorama Elite' in the previous picture. This vehicle carries the 'Townsend Thoresen Holidays' livery of orange and white which is also carried by five other vehicles of similar design in the Southdown fleet. Townsend Thoresen operate south coast ferry services from Dover to Calais and Zeebrugge and from Portsmouth and Southampton to Le Havre and Cherbourg.
Andrew Kennedy

Plate 211: Fifty convertible open top bodies to fit Bristol VRT chassis for the National Bus Company subsidiaries were built by Eastern Coachworks at Lowestoft. These vehicles have facing seats at the front and removable roofs. Thirty of these joined the Southdown fleet and ten were fitted with double doorways. On 25th June 198_ No. 615 (UWV 615S) is seen on Brighton se_ front running empty in an eastboun_ direction. It is noticeable that the board di_ played on the front of the vehicle indicat_ the open topper is not 'one-man-operated' as are the VRs in general. Of the remaini_ 20 'convertible' VRs, eleven were purchased by Western National, six going to Hants _ Dorset and three were bought by Sou_ Wales Transport. In 1979 the six Hants _ Dorset convertible 'open toppers' we_ exchanged with Southern Vectis for co_ ventional Bristol VRs. By 1981 only 49 _ these vehicles remained in service, as N_ 597 of the Southdown fleet was destroy_ by fire, together with thirteen other doub_ deckers at Conway Street garage, Hove, _ 14th April 1978. Three more vehicles we_ seriously damaged.

*Dave Sava_*

Plate 212: A 1970 Marshall bodied Bris_ RESL, No. 487 (TCD 487J), of the Southdo_ fleet, stops to take on more fares at Bright_ on 24th April 1981. The significant differen_ between the Marshall bodied RE can be co_ pared with the ECW bodied version in **Plate** _. Preparing to pull out from behind this vehicle_ a blue and white liveried Brighton Borou_ Transport Leyland Atlantean, No. _ (JFG 362N), with an East Lancs body.

Geoff M._

Plate 213: Advertising the Brighton Travel card and displaying the British Rail logo, Southdown 1972 dual-doored Bristol VRT, No. 538 (WUF 538K), fitted with a Series I ECW body, cautiously negotiates a busy area of Brighton on 8th May 1981. This is the only vehicle in the Southdown fleet carrying this livery, although another Bristol VR, No. 510 (UUF 110J), advertises the Portsmouth Area Travel card. Two brackets are clearly visible on the front of the vehicle for the purpose of displaying instruction boards, similar to the one in **Plate 211**. However, the 'Pay As You Enter' sign on this vehicle is in the form of a sticker located between the two brackets. Similar fittings can be seen on other vehicles portrayed in this section on Southdown.

Dave Savage

SOUTHERN VECTIS

Plate 214: The bus station at Ryde on the Isle of Wight is situated on the forecourt of Ryde Esplanade railway station, and is a matter of a few yards away from where the hovercraft arrives and departs for Southsea. With all four travel facilities, rail, boat, hovercraft and bus services on the Island, this location is the centre for visitors to the Isle of Wight. Most towns and villages on the Island can be reached by Southern Vectis buses from Ryde bus station, and on 7th November 1981, a Southern Vectis Leyland National Mk. 1, No. 885 (ODL 885R), leaves for Haylands, inland, on the outskirts of Ryde. A Bristol VR on a Cowes service stands at the rear. The name 'Rydabus' carried by the Leyland National was introduced in December 1978, but not as a result of an M.A.P. survey. The differing pod designs fitted to Leyland National buses can clearly be seen in this view. No. 885, a 10.3 metre version, is fitted with the shorter higher pod introduced in 1975, whilst to the right of the picture, the Leyland National, only partially seen, carries the old style longer flatter pod. The variable vents on the pod are also noticeable.

Rex Kennedy

Plate 215: A Southern Vectis 1967 Bristol RESL6G, No. 810 (HDL 25E), with 43 seat ECW bodywork, sits amongst some of its newer stablemates in the yard adjoining Ryde garage on 7th November 1981. This vehicle is one of three of its kind in the Southern Vectis fleet and together with Nos. 809 and 811, is one of the oldest single deck vehicles in the fleet.

Andrew Kennedy

Plate 216: An 11.3 metre version of the Leyland National, No. 872 (XDL 796L), in the Southern Vectis fleet, stands at Ryde bus garage on 7th November 1981. In 1973 when Southern Vectis took their first Leyland Nationals, they received five 10.3 metre models, the first five produced for a NBC subsidiary. Southern Vectis were the sole customer for the short 10.3 metre version at the initial stage of Leyland National production.
Rex Kennedy

Plate 217: To commemorate the Golden Jubilee of Southern Vectis operation (1929-1979), a Bristol VRT, No. 650 (MDL 650R), was repainted early in 1979 in the pre-1931 livery of blue with red lining, red window surrounds and a white roof. On 14th June 1981 this vehicle was seen leaving Ryde bus station for Yarmouth with a fairly full complement. The name 'Vectis' can be seen on the side of the vehicle. This livery, carried by the VRT, was never seen on double deck vehicles, as at the time the livery was originally in use, the 'Vectis' fleet consisted solely of single deckers.
Colin Caddy

Plate 218: Fountain Coaches are part of the Southern Vectis organisation. No. 125 (ODL 176R), a Bedford YMT with Duple bodywork photographed at Yarmouth Ferry on the Isle of Wight on 14th June 1981, carries the orange and cream livery familiar to these coaches. In 1967 Fountain Coaches were taken over by Shamrock & Rambler and now retain the old livery of that company. In 1969 Shamrock & Rambler relinquished their interests on the Isle of Wight which resulted in Fountain Coaches being placed under the ownership of Southern Vectis.
Colin Caddy

Plate 219: Bound for home on the Isle of Wight, a Southern Vectis 1977 Bedford YMT, No. 418 (ODL 175R), with Duple bodywork and in white NBC coach livery, passes through the wooded area around Winslade, south of Basingstoke on the Alton road, on Sunday 18th October 1981. On its destination blind it carries the identical number to its fleet number. Southern Vectis operate a predominance of Bedfords in their coach fleet, the majority with Duple bodywork, others being Plaxton and Willowbrook bodied.

Andrew Kennedy

Plate 220: A withdrawn Southern Vectis Bristol LHS, No. 835 (NDL 771G), with a Marshall 35 seat body, stands at Ryde garage on 7th November 1981. Southern Vectis started the trend with this design of Bristol LHS, and this particular vehicle was withdrawn from service before the 1981 summer season. By the end of 1981 all the Southern Vectis Marshall bodied LHS vehicles had been withdrawn. At the rear stands a Bristol FS6G, No. 565 (TDL 998), a vehicle over 20 years old. This vehicle now carries a yellow band between the upper and lower decks and is occasionally used for driver training. Ryde garage is one of five garages on the Isle of Wight operated by Southern Vectis. An outstation also exists at Cowes which is used by Fountain Coaches.

Andrew Kennedy

SOUTH WALES
DE CYMRU

Plate 221: Port Talbot's industrial environment is portrayed in this view, as a South Wales Transport Ford R1014, with Duple Dominant bus bodywork, returns children home with a School Bus service on 24th November 1981. The local identity name 'Afanway' was introduced in June 1980 on vehicles operating in Port Talbot and the Afan Valley areas. This vehicle is one of 17 delivered in 1976 having this design of body by Duple Coachworks, this picture giving a good profile view of its style. Completing that original 1976 delivery of 50 Ford R1014 Duple Dominants placed by NBC, East Yorkshire, Eastern National, Lincolnshire, Oxford/South Midland and United Counties shared the balance.

Rex Kennedy

Plate 222: A South Wales Leyland National, No. 745 (GCY 745N), leaves the little South Wales village of Blaengwrach, near Glyn Neath, on 24th November 1981, with a service for Hirwaun where it will connect with another service for Merthyr Tydfil. The vehicle is fitted with the newer style heating and ventilation pod and is an 11.3 metre version. The typical Welsh mountainous area in the rear of the view reaches a height of over 1,700 feet, and directly behind the Leyland National stand the remains of the railway bridge which once carried the line from Aberdare to Neath.

Rex Kennedy

Plate 223: Llanelli South Wales Transport garage still has signs of the days when trams graced the town. An ex-East Kent Leyland National, No. 1066, now in the South Wales fleet as No. 823 (NFN 66M), receives attention inside the garage on 25th August 1981. South Wales Transport acquired eight of these vehicles from East Kent late in 1980. Whilst in the East Kent fleet these 11.3 metre Leyland Nationals were fitted with 49 seats, and on arrival in South Wales and prior to entering service, they were converted to carry 52 seats. Of the eight vehicles concerned, the majority are allocated to Llanelli garage.

Rex Kennedy

Plate 224: South Wales Transport ran the last AEC double deckers within the NBC fleet. Pictured at Swansea bus station in August 1981, No. 889 (GWN 867E), one of the last five AEC Regent V vehicles to survive until the end of 1981, all with Willowbrook bodies, stood parked with more modern double deckers in the South Wales fleet. The other four were Nos. 861, 869, 881 and 886. Sadly the last of these five vehicles was withdrawn from service on 3rd January 1982. The 'Regent V' was used on the Swansea to Pennard route, as the tight turn at Plough Corner, Bishopston on the Gower Peninsula, prevented the use of other vehicles in the South Wales fleet. This service, No. 14, is now operated by Bedford YMQ midibuses, a vast contrast to the popular Regent V. Withdrawal of South Wales Regent V double deckers commenced in 1966, one year before the last one was delivered. Only four now remain in stock, two as towing vehicles, one driver trainer and the other as an office at Gorseinon. The end of another era.

Brian Jackson

Plate 225: The South Wales garage at Pontardawe is overlooked by mountains on both sides as it sits in the Swansea Valley. This garage has an allocation of approximately 30 vehicles, including Leyland Nationals, Bristol VRs, Bristol REs and Ford R1014s. One of the Ford R1014 vehicles, No. 265 (NCY 265R), with Duple Dominant bus bodywork, stood at the rear of Pontardawe garage on 25th August 1981. This was one of the batch of seventeen delivered to South Wales between August and November 1976. South Wales Transport also operated Ford R1014 vehicles with Willowbrook bodies which have now almost completely disappeared.

Rex Kennedy

Plate 226: The comparatively new bus station at Port Talbot is of the 'sawtooth' or 'end on' design favoured by NBC in certain towns, where all facilities such as enquiry offices and waiting rooms are built on one platform area. Unfortunately, as reversing of buses prior to departure is necessary, locations with services more frequent than half-hourly cannot operate this style of bus station. There is also a certain amount of accident risk, hence the instructive notices at the entrance to this bus station. At Port Talbot, the 'facility building' still awaited completion at the time this picture was taken on 24th November 1981. A South Wales Bedford YMQ, No. 280 (FCY 280W), fitted with a Duple body and 45 dual-purpose seats, leaves this bus station, which is situated between the Glamorgan mountains and Swansea Bay, on a Llanelli service. This vehicle was new to South Wales in October 1980, and is one of seven dual purpose versions. This company also operate eleven of this type of vehicle fitted with normal bus seats. The YMQ was introduced by Bedford to replace the YLQ in 1980.

Andrew Kennedy

Plate 227: The two Welsh NBC companies which operate in South Wales, National Welsh and South Wales Transport, carry their company names in Welsh on the offside of their vehicles. A 'De Cymru' South Wales Transport 1975 AEC Reliance, No. 160 (HCY 468N), fitted with Duple Dominant coachwork and painted in semi-coach livery, loads at Cardiff bus station with an X1 service for Swansea on 14th July 1981. This vehicle once carried the fleet number 468 and was renumbered, in April 1981, during a minor renumbering scheme within the company. Carefully passing by, a National Welsh (Cymru Cenedlaethol) Bristol VRT, in full 'National Holidays' advertising livery, No. HR 1777 (SKG 896S), prepares to pull in to take passengers up the Taff Vale to Pontypridd and Maerdy. This livery appears on Bristol VRs in the NBC fleet throughout Britain, often with a blue and white 'clouded sky' roof. This bus station is situated outside the Cardiff Central railway station.

Rex Kennedy

Plate 228: The South Wales Transport garage at Port Talbot was once the home of Thomas Bros. (Port Talbot) Ltd., a company originally formed in June 1951. Thomas Bros., together with Neath & Cardiff Luxury Coaches Ltd. and United Welsh were absorbed into the South Wales Transport (NBC) fleet in 1971, but prior to this carried no fleet numbers. In the late afternoon of 24th November 1981, a South Wales Transport 1974 Ford Transit 16 seater Strachan bodied minibus, No. 99 (VYM 502M), stood in the back of this garage. This vehicle was acquired from City of Oxford Motor Services in 1977 where it carried the fleet number 705. Prior to this, the minibus was under the ownership of National Travel (South East). In December 1980, South Wales withdrew No. 99 from passenger service, and by mid-1981 it was used as a staff vehicle for Port Talbot garage. In the yard outside this spacious garage stands another service vehicle, No. 54 (999 BCY), a 1962 AEC Regent V with Willowbrook body, renumbered from service vehicle No. 6 and prior to that, when in service, it carried the fleet numbers 764 and 564. This vehicle has seen a variety of liveries including dark red, poppy red and NBC 'trainee' yellow. Beside the 'trainer' is South Wales No. 460 (UCY 979J), an ex-Neath & Cardiff Luxury Coaches 1970 Plaxton bodied AEC Reliance, acquired by South Wales at the takeover of this company in 1971 and now in a dual purpose livery, bearing no resemblance to the attractive brown and red livery of N. & C. Coaches.

Rex Kennedy

Plate 229: Taking out the 136 service to Porthcawl on 24th November 1981, a South Wales 'Express West' coach pulls away from Port Talbot bus station. 'Express West' was a new limited stop service using the M4 motorway, which was introduced jointly by South Wales Transport, National Welsh and Bristol Omnibus Co. on 19th September 1981. Three routes are scheduled for these coaches, X10, a two hourly service from Bristol to Cardiff, Swansea and Carmarthen, via Llanelli, and X11/12, also two hourly, between X10 services to Haverfordwest. This, of course, results in a fast hourly service from Bristol to Swansea. At Carmarthen the X11/12 divides with the X11 continuing its journey on to Haverfordwest via Narberth and the X12 going to Tenby, Pembroke and Pembroke Dock. The single fare of £2.90 from Bristol to Haverfordwest is extremely competitive, and the 75 minute journey from Bristol to Cardiff costs only £1.50 single or £1.75 day return. The 'Express West' livery of red and blue stripes tapering towards the rear of the vehicle is very attractive and is clearly visible on 1977 Leyland Leopard PSU3, No. 169 (RWN 477S), with Duple body, seen in this view.

Rex Kennedy

EXPRESSWEST

TRENT

Plate 230: The large cotton mill built in 1912 and situated at the north end of Belper, lies at the road junction to Matlock and Ashbourne. Trent Motor Traction operate regular services into Belper from both these locations, and on 26th November 1981 a dual purpose 1974 Bristol RELH, No. 286 (NCH 769M), heads into town from the direction of Matlock. Belper's Trent garage has an allocation of approximately 20 vehicles of which this is one. On careful scrutiny of this bus, the fleet number can be seen, unusually situated, on the offside front corner of the vehicle, about 9in. from the bottom.

Rex Kennedy

Plate 231: A Trent Daimler Fleetline, No. 552 (NRC 52K), with ECW bodywork, passes the bus station at Derby, on the inner ring road, on 18th September 1981. The vehicle in this view is one of nineteen of its type purchased in 1972, eight of which were destroyed by fire at Nottingham's Trent garage in December 1977. No. 558 has now been withdrawn from service, and the allocation of the remaining ten of these vehicles is shared between Nottingham and Derby, the two major centres.

Rex Kennedy

Plate 232: Passing carefully through the roadworks at Matlock on 26th November 1981, a Trent Bristol RELL, No. 343 (LRC 343K), with ECW bodywork, proceeds towards the bus station before continuing on to Bakewell. This vehicle was ordered by the North Western Road Car Co. prior to terminating their operations in late 1971, but entered service with Trent in 1972.

Andrew Kennedy

Plate 233: Ex-North Western Road Car Co. 1971 Bristol RELL, with Marshall bodywork, now in the Trent fleet and carrying the fleet number 340 (SJA 355K), heads through Darley Dale towards Matlock on 26th November 1981 en route for Derby. This vehicle was added to the North Western fleet in this company's last year of existence as a bus operator along with 53 others. The old North Western fleet number of Trent No. 340, was No. 355, similar to its registration number. On the demise of the North Western Road Car Co. in 1972, 13 of their vehicles joined the Trent fleet with others going to Crosville and SELNEC. At the time of the North Western take-over, in March of that year, Trent expanded their services based on the ex-North Western garages at Buxton and Matlock.

Rex Kennedy

Plate 235: Langley Mill, situated between Heanor and Eastwood, is the location of one of the larger Trent Motor Traction garages. As Trent Leyland National, No. 499 (XAL 499S), pictured here, proceeds down the slope from the summit of the bridge at Langley Mill en route to New Eastwood on Thursday, 26th November 1981, it prepares to pick up more fares from the bus stop situated just outside the Trent garage. Langley Mill is one of the four largest garages in the Trent network, the others being at Derby, Nottingham and Alfreton.

Rex Kennedy

Plate 234: The picturesque inland resort of Matlock Bath, usually crowded with day trippers and holidaymakers in the summer, is one of the more photogenic spots within the Trent Motor Traction network. On 26th November 1981 a Bristol RELL, No. 345 (LRC 345K), fitted with ECW bodywork, makes its way along the side of the River Derwent after leaving the town of Matlock en route for Millers Green. This Bristol RE was ordered by the North Western Road Car Co. together with four other similar vehicles, and was licenced by Trent before entering service in 1972. North Western ceased bus operations at the end of 1971. At the top of the hill in the background, which is known as the 'Heights of Abraham' and at a height of approximately 800ft., is the Victoria Prospect Tower, affording magnificent views over the Derwent Valley.

Rex Kennedy

Trent Bus Stations

Plate 236: The Trent garage at Belper also doubles as a bus station, with single deck vehicles entering from the rear of the garage and down a fairly narrow tunnel into the main part of the building. The maintenance bay and entrance are at the rear of the garage and are on a higher level to the area on view in this picture. On 26th November 1981, a Trent Leyland National Mk. 1, No. 456 (PRR 456R), awaits departure for Derby, whilst beyond, a 1978 Leyland Leopard dual purpose coach, No. 131 (ARB 131T), with Plaxton bodywork, prepares to leave for Ripley. At the rear of the garage two more Leyland Nationals, No. 464 (RTO 464R) and No. 419 (XRB 419L), stand off duty. No. 419 is an ex-Midland General vehicle acquired by Trent in the take-over of this company on 1st October 1976.

Andrew Kennedy

Plate 237: Matlock bus station, now predominantly Trent, was once a North Western Road Car Co. location. This bus station is also used by East Midland vehicles and the independent operator, Hulley's. The design of Matlock bus station is of the 'through platform' type with basic shelters and provides vehicles with space to pass others already picking up passengers. On 26th November 1981, a Trent Leyland National, No. 477 (VCH 477S), awaits departure for Alfreton and Mansfield. Bristol RE No. 343 (LRC 343K) passes a Hulley's vehicle on the right of this picture. This bus station nestles beneath the hilly residential area of Matlock.

Rex Kennedy

Plate 238: The unusual two way half moon bus station at Derby sees a variety of vehicles including those of Trent Motor Traction, Derby City Transport and Felix Bus Services. On 18th September 1981, a Trent Leyland Leopard, No. 114 (PRA 114R), with Alexander 'T' type bodywork and painted in the all-white NBC coach livery, stands at one of the pick up points. This vehicle received its all-white livery in July 1980, where other vehicles of this design in the Trent fleet carry the dual-purpose livery. The rear of a Leyland Leopard, No. 328 (LCH 328K), with Marshall bodywork, also in the Trent fleet, is on view. This vehicle is the sole survivor of this particular batch delivered in 1972.

Rex Kennedy

Market Day at Ilkeston

Plate 239: Market day at Ilkeston provides a setting with a difference as a Trent Leyland National, No. 481 (XAL 481S), slowly moves down the hill after picking up more passengers in the town, before continuing its journey to Nottingham on 26th November 1981. This vehicle is one of the dual-doored 44 seat versions of the Leyland National, and is one of over 60 in the Trent fleet.
Andrew Kennedy

Plate 240: Ilkeston has the distinction of having both an NBC Trent garage and a Barton Transport garage situated in close proximity to one another. This 'market day' view on 26th November 1981 shows locally allocated Trent Bristol RELL, No 366 (ORB 253K), which was an ex Midland General vehicle prior to its transfer to Trent on 1st October 1976. The open area around the corner, to the left of the picture beside the church, is used as a picking up point by Barton buses. The town of Ilkeston is known for its light industries producing lace and hosiery.
Rex Kennedy

UNITED

Plate 241: The town of Stockton stands at the mouth of the River Tees directly opposite Thornaby. The wide one-way high street is clearly seen in this view on a market day, in September 1981, together with the collection of bus stops used by various bus operators. Whilst a Cleveland Transit Leyland Fleetline, No. H126 (GAJ 126V), with Northern Counties bodywork, picks up more fares, it is passed by a United 1980 Willowbrook bodied Leyland Leopard, No. 6225 (TPT 25V), in dual purpose livery en route for Billingham-on-Tees. Another operator in this town, as can be seen from the nearest bus stop, is Eden Bus Services. A variety of liveries are regularly on view in Stockton, the poppy red of United buses combining with the green and yellow buses of Cleveland Transit and the red and cream of Eden Motor Services. The Cleveland Transit coaches and midibuses are painted in orange and primrose. Cleveland Transit was formed in 1974 and prior to this date was Tees-side Municipal Transport. There is no United garage at Stockton, the nearest being at Middlesbrough with an allocation of approximately 60 vehicles.

Kevin Lane

Plate 242: United buses use the cobbled market place, at Thirsk in North Yorkshire, as the town bus station. On 14th November 1981 a Ripon based United 1979 Bristol LH, No. 1705 (LPT 705T), fitted with a 43 seat ECW body, awaits departure for Northallerton, beside the old clock tower. This vehicle carries the fleet number on a white plastic plate above the driver's window, a system used only by United. The Bristol LH vehicle first appeared on the bus scene in 1967 as a successor to the SU type. The LH seen in this view is of the long chassis variety, whereas the one seen in **Plate 116** in the London Country fleet is fitted to a short chassis with the 7ft. 6in. narrower body.

Rex Kennedy

Plate 243: A vast shortage of buses was experienced by Sheffield during the early months of 1981, which resulted in the loan of many vehicles from NBC subsidiaries such as Ribble, United, West Yorkshire and West Riding, in addition to some from Nottingham, Derby, Leicester and Hull Corporations together with Greater Manchester and Tyne & Wear PTEs. During their use in Sheffield, these vehicles carried temporary South Yorkshire PTE fleet numbers in addition to those of their parent company. On 30th October 1981, a United Bristol RELL, No. 5002 (EHN 602J), also bearing the South Yorkshire PTE fleet number 2018, works the 'City Clipper' service in Sheffield and is seen passing through Fitzalan Square. The 'City Clipper' service in Sheffield was previously operated by 10 M.A.N. and Leyland articulated buses each with a combined total seating and standing capacity greater than that of a standard double decker bus. United's No. 5002 together with 5034 and 5035 were loaned to South Yorkshire PTE in mid-September 1981 after the articulated single deckers had been taken out of service.

Adrian Foster

Plate 244: With the many independent bus operators using the bus station at Durham, many unusual bus designs frequent this fine city, but none more unusual than this Plaxton Panorama bodied Leyland Leopard L2 towing vehicle in NBC's United fleet. This particular vehicle, No. 1168 (821 YEH), pictured on 26th July 1981, prior to acquisition in 1976 by United Automobile Services, was owned by Ribble together with No. 1169 (822 YEH) of the United fleet, and was purchased by them at the same time. These two vehicles (ex-Ribble Nos. 1060 and 1061) were built in 1963 and in that year were purchased by Ribble from the Michelin Tyre Company in Stoke-on-Trent, the original owners. These vehicles were originally fitted with 41 seats and No. 1169 is no longer in the United fleet.

Dave Savage

NATIONAL EXPRESS

Plate 245: The northbound service area at Trowell, on the M1 motorway, is often used as a refreshment stop for long distance coaches travelling to Yorkshire and north-east England. The 201 National Express service from London (Victoria) to Newcastle upon Tyne breaks its journey at Trowell on 13th September 1981, before moving on to its next and last stop before Newcastle, this being Darlington bus station. On this occasion, three vehicles were en route for Newcastle upon Tyne, the two in NBC white coach livery being Nos. 1070 (WHA 235H) and 1071 (WHA 237H), once under the ownership of Midland Red. These two 1970 Plaxton bodied Leyland Leopards, classified C11 by Midland Red, were acquired by United in May 1981, together with two similar vehicles. In the United fleet they carry the fleet numbers 1070–1073 and were numbered, 6235, 6237, 6238 and 6241 when owned by Midland Red.

Rex Kennedy

Plate 246: United followed Northern General in repainting a number of vehicles in a variation of the Tyne & Wear PTE livery following Tyneside reorganisation. This livery was restricted to United vehicles working in the Newcastle upon Tyne area, and on 24th July 1981, No. 702 (UGR 702R), a 1976 Bristol VRT makes its way through Newcastle in its deep yellow and white livery. Following further reorganisation on Tyneside on 22nd November 1981, service 87, being operated by the vehicle pictured here, came under the control of Tyne & Wear PTE, whereas previously it was worked jointly by the PTE and United Automobile Services.

Dave Savage

Plate 247: Wending its way through the heavily congested streets of Newcastle upon Tyne, a United Leyland National Mk. 1, No. 3049 (ABR 861S), resplendent in its Tyne & Wear deep yellow and white livery, works a local service on 24th July 1981. This vehicle is of particular interest as it carries the Tyne & Wear Transport fleetname on the side together with the NBC symbol. Leyland Nationals make up, with a total of just under 160, approximately 35% of the United single deck bus fleet.

Dave Savage

Plate 248: By the end of 1981, United Automobile Services operated just one open-top double decker on sea-front duties at the north east coastal resort of Scarborough. This open-topper, No. 650 (OCS 590H), is an ex-Western SMT vehicle and is pictured in August 1981 picking up holidaymakers, some already braving the east coast bracing air on the upper deck. The apparent emptiness of the lower deck indicates vastly the attraction of these specially adapted vehicles. The livery carried by No. 650 is white with a shocking pink band at the top, with varying shades of blue bands at the bottom of the vehicle body. This 1969 Bristol VR, with ECW bodywork, was acquired from the Scottish company in 1973, but was not converted to open-top until 1981. Other vehicles converted in a similar manner, also purchased from Scottish operators, were No. 636 (ex-Central SMT), No. 637 (ex-Eastern Scottish) and Nos. 642 and 644 (ex-Western SMT). All these vehicles were part of the massive exchange of 242 vehicles which took place from 1971 to 1974 between Scottish and English operators, resulting in the Scottish Bus Group acquiring Bristol FLF Lodekkas from Eastern Counties, Southern Vectis, Southdown, Alder Valley, Eastern National, Northern General, Lincolnshire and United. Until 1981 all open-top vehicles operating in Scarborough were painted in a green livery.

Geoff Coxon

Plate 249: A 43 seat 1974 Bristol LH6L, No. 1610 (AHN 610M), of the United fleet, leaves the town of Sedgefield with a service to Stanley in September 1981. The service route 68 follows a long semi-circular trail from Stockton-on-Tees westward to Crook and then north-east to Stanley, the nearest town to the now growing Beamish open air museum where the north-east's past way of life is beautifully portrayed. There are at Beamish furnished pit cottages, a colliery complex, a railway area and a working tramcar, plus many other interesting exhibits.

Kevin Lane

Plate 250: A red and white liveried United Bristol RELH, No. 6093 (BHN 693N), leaves the bus station at Newcastle upon Tyne on 19th June 1981. The Bristol RELH carries a high chassis frame with a level floor, differing from the RELL low chassis version which has the floor sloping down to a very low level front entrance door as seen in **Plate 187**. Production of the Bristol RE ceased in the late 1970s with the two Northern Ireland operators, Ulsterbus and Citybus, placing the last orders.

Rex Kennedy

UNITED COUNTIES

Plate 251: The ultra-modern city of Milton Keynes provides excellent shopping facilities incorporating ample parking and attracts visitors from miles around. Frequent bus services operate in the area picking up and setting down passengers directly outside the Central Milton Keynes shopping area. On 5th December 1981, Christmas shoppers return home as they board United Counties 11.6 metre Leyland National Mk. 2, No. 584 (NRP 584V), en route for Wolverton. This vehicle was delivered to United Counties in June 1980 and carries the local identity name 'Citybus'.

Rex Kennedy

Plate 252: On 31st December 1981, one of the new Leyland Olympian double deckers in the United Counties fleet, No. 615 (ARP 615X), diverted to United Counties from a Southdown order, stops in High Street South, Dunstable to pick up more fares as it works a local Downside-Houghton Regis-Luton service. This vehicle is allocated to Luton garage and came into the United Counties fleet in December 1981. The first Olympians, Nos. 601-603, entered service with United Counties in November 1981 after delivery in August, having been originally ordered by Alder Valley. A prototype of the Leyland Olympian commenced trials with Ribble in August 1980, and the production model permits maximum speeds up to 47 m.p.h. and a climbing ability to cope with a 1 in 3½ gradient.

Kevin Lane

Bristol VRs

Plate 253: The market square at St. Neots, Cambridgeshire, is used as the town bus station for United Counties and is also used as a coach stop for through NBC express services. On 25th November 1981, No. 750 (RRP 750G), the very first Bristol VR purchased by United Counties, stands at this location prior to continuing its duties. This vehicle is a 1969 Series I Bristol VR with the 'T' route indicator panel and flat windscreen. Since 1972 curved windscreens have been fitted to Bristol VR double deckers. During 1981 two Series I Bristol VRs in the United Counties fleet have been rebodied with Series 3 VR bodies. These were Nos. 755 (TBD 755G) in September and 752 (RRP 752G) in December.
Rex Kennedy

Plate 254: A 1973 United Counties Series 2 ECW bodied Bristol VRT, No. 800 (JRP 800L), stands by the wash at Bletchley garage on 28th January 1981. The white livery, advertising 'Cityrider' tickets in Milton Keynes, was given to this vehicle in July 1979. However, in August 1981, four Bristol VR double deckers in the United Counties fleet, including No. 800, were painted in the original 1921 livery of this company, with dark blue lower deck panels, red upper deck panels and white roof, white bands and window surrounds. This livery commemorates 60 years of public transport by the United Counties Omnibus Co. Ltd. The other three vehicles in this livery are Nos. 828 (HBD 165N), 829 (HBD 166N) and 834 (HRP 674N).
Geoff Mills

Plate 255: The spacious interior of the United Counties garage at Kettering shows another Bristol VR of that fleet, No. 889 (XNV 889S), minus a panel beneath the driver's window, on 26th August 1981. A collection of differing designs can be seen in the distance over the inspection pits. United Counties use a system of coloured plates behind the fleet numbers on their buses to indicate the allocation of the vehicle. In this case No. 889 is on a yellow background which relates to Kettering garage. At about this time approximately 40 United Counties vehicles were allocated to Kettering. The unusual National Express advertisement on the side of this vehicle is clearly portrayed.
Rex Kennedy

Plate 256: On a warm 16th May 1981, a United Counties Bristol VR, No. 930 (SNV 930W), climbs to the summit of the railway bridge in Bedford, which once passed over the railway line which ran from Bletchley to Cambridge, and now only continues east as far as an industrial site just beyond the United Counties bus garage. As one stands on this bridge, the Bedford St. John's railway station can be seen below on the one side, with the NBC bus garage on the other. Bedford town centre lies in the distance. No. 930 was delivered new to United Counties in August 1980.

Rex Kennedy

Plate 257: One of the longer double deck routes in the United Counties network is the one from Aylesbury to Luton. In the summer of 1981 a United Counties Bristol VR, No. 918 (HBD 918T), in the all-over National Holidays livery, takes on even more passengers to add to its already heavily laden payload as it stops at Tring. The bus stop pictured in this view is also used by NBC 'Greenline' vehicles. No. 918 was painted in this livery in July 1981 and shows the blue and white 'cloudy sky' roof differing from the National Holidays advertiser in **Plate 227**. This vehicle is also the only Bristol VR in the United Counties fleet fitted with coach seating.

Kevin Lane

Plate 258: United Counties have used a variety of designs of midibuses and minibuses within their fleet over the years. They range from the 15 seat Deansgate bodied Mercedes of which they purchased six in 1975, to the latest Lex bodied Bedford YMQ now running in Leighton Buzzard. Other designs acquired include two Mercedes with 24 seater Chartaway bodies, a 12 seat Ford Transit minibus from Tricentrol, and in 1980, a 12 seat Ford Transit with a Dormobile body. All the Mercedes vehicles were, in December 1979, allocated to Bletchley garage and Ford Transit No. 70 (TVD 851R), used as the Lilbourne Community Bus in the Northampton area, was replaced in 1981 by No. 71 (OKV 531W), another 12 seater Ford Transit. Another design used was the Ford with Tricentrol midibus bodywork pictured here entering High Street, Leighton Buzzard, in February 1981, working a local town service. No. 071 (PKX 271R) carries a combined United Counties and Bedfordshire County Council fleetname, although only on hire from Tricentrol together with No. 072 at the time. The midibus service in Leighton Buzzard was introduced in September 1976.

Kevin Lane

Midibuses — United Counties Style

Plate 259: The latest additions to the United Counties midibus fleet are three shortened Bedford YMQ versions with Lex bodywork. These Bedfords, whose bodies were shortened by Tricentrol, replaced the Ford vehicles previously used on Leighton Buzzard town services. On 14th May 1981, during its first week of service, midibus No. 52 (WNH 52W), leaves the town centre sporting its fine green and white livery.

Kevin Lane

Plate 260: Bad weather conditions invariably result in a build up of traffic as motorists and commercial vehicles carefully negotiate the hazardous conditions. After one of the many snowstorms faced by Britain in December 1981, a United Counties 1968 dual-doored Bristol RELL, No. 371 (PXE 111F), ex-Luton Corporation No. 111, fights its way through the slush in Dunstable with a local service on 8th December 1981. Luton Corporation ceased bus operation in 1970, resulting in United Counties taking Leyland Titans, Albion Lowlanders, Dennis Lolines and Bristol REs into their fleet. Whilst in the Luton Corporation fleet these vehicles were in a livery of red with a cream trim.

Kevin Lane

Plate 261: Greyfriars bus station at Northampton is used by United Counties the local Northampton Transport buses, Midland Red vehicles and London Country (Greenline) coaches operating the 760 Northampton to Heathrow Airport service. In addition to these companies, National Express coaches pick up as they pass through the town. On 26th August 1981, a United Counties Bristol VR, No. 936 (SNV 936W), pulls away from the bus station in Northampton en route for Rushden. United Counties operate over 200 Bristol VR double deckers in their fleet, and since the last Bristol VR was outshopped from the manufacturers in mid-August 1981, United Counties are taking Leyland Olympians, the successor to the VR. Standing in the bus station can be seen the rear of United Counties trainee vehicle No. 1007, (KBD 716D), a 1966 Bristol FS6G which, when in service, carried the fleet number 716. This scene portrays fourteen years of Bristol ECW design of double deckers.

Rex Kennedy

Plate 262: A 1971 dual purpose Bristol RELH, No. 213 (YRP 213J), with ECW bodywork and fitted out with semi-coach seating, lies parked at Kettering bus station on 26th August 1981. Off duty vehicles are parked at this location on the far side of the bus station away from the picking up points, and the whole area is on an elevated section overlooking the United Counties garage. Bristol were the first British commercial vehicle manufacturer to put a single deck passenger chassis into production with a rear under-floor engine, this of course was the Bristol RE.

Rex Kennedy

Willowbrooks

Plate 263: A Leyland Leopard United Counties PSU3 coach, No. 241 (KVV 241V), fitted with Willowbrook bodywork, pulls out of Bletchley bus station in the spring of 1981 with a service for London. The Willowbrook 'W' emblem is clearly visible on the radiator grille. A clear view of the 'Citybus' local identity name used in the Bletchley area is seen at the rear of a United Counties Bristol RE standing in the bus station.
Kevin Lane

Plate 264: Aylesbury bus station is situated beneath a new shopping area giving under-cover accommodation for waiting travellers. During its last month of service, a United Counties 1974 Bedford YRT, No. 113 (RBD 113M), with Willowbrook bodywork, prepares to leave Aylesbury as it loads up for Cheddington on a wet evening in January 1981. By the end of 1981, all the Willowbrook bodied Bedford YRT and YRQ vehicles had been withdrawn from the United Counties fleet.
Kevin Lane

Plate 265: Lines of withdrawn United Counties vehicles both single and double deck, lie at the rear of Wellingborough garage in a disposal yard on 26th August 1981. A variation of old designs can be seen at this location and in this view a 1974 Bedford YRT, ex-No. 111 (RBD 111M), with a Willowbrook body, having had its United Counties fleetname obliterated, stands beside a 1966 United Counties Bristol FS double decker, ex-No. 710 (HBD 710D). The Willowbrook was withdrawn from service in March 1981 and the Bristol FS in November 1980. A fire in the Wellingborough disposal yard on 26th November 1979 resulted in three ex-Courtline of Luton Plaxton bodied Fords being destroyed. Vehicles slightly damaged included another ex-Courtline Ford Plaxton, together with a Bristol FLF and four ex-Luton Corporation Bristol RELL single deckers which were due for collection by a dealer.
Rex Kennedy

WESTERN NATIONAL

Plate 266: The driver of ECW bodied Western National 1973 Bristol LH, No. 1597 (NFJ 597M), goes through the long routine of taking fares at Taunton bus station on 20th October 1981. Of course in cases where many of the travellers hold weekly, monthly or season tickets, this operation is speeded up. On this occasion the majority of the passengers appear to be shoppers, who have the added problem of putting down their purchases before paying their fares and finding a seat. Taunton bus station is situated in the town centre, whereas the garage is out on the A38 Bridgwater road.

Andrew Kennedy

Plate 267: A 1970 Western National Bristol RELH, No. 1473 (RDV 424H), fitted with dual purpose seats, arrives at St. Austell bus station prior to leaving for Bodmin on 7th April 1981. This bus station is conveniently situated adjacent to the railway station, and a frequent flow of bus services can be seen at this location. The local identity name 'Cornish Fairways' seen above the windows of this vehicle, was introduced in May 1980 on buses operating from Western National garages in mid and West Cornwall, but this time not as the result of an M.A.P. survey. In the distance is a Western National Truro-bound 1976 Leyland National Mk. 1, No. 2822 (MOD 822P), carrying the 'Cornish Fairways' name on the front. It is noticeable that the fleetname 'Western National' is not displayed on either of these vehicles.

Rex Kennedy

Plate 268: Prior to November 1969 the outskirts of Sherborne was Southern National territory, and on 23rd April 1981 a Leyland National Mk. 1, No. 2824 (MOD 824P), stops to pick up a fare before continuing its journey through the Dorset byways. A rural scene very typical of bus operation in this part of Britain.

Graham Wise

Plate 269: The now Western National garage at Yeovil was also once in the Southern National network, and this view of Leyland National No 2812 (HTA 843N), a 49 seat version, shows the vehicle lying at the rear of the garage on 4th April 1981, having had its wheels removed. Prior to the use of the M4 motorway for the daily express services from London to Exeter via Salisbury and Yeovil, the old route from Victoria coach station to Exeter, Plymouth and Cornwall took the A30 trunk road using Yeovil as a refreshment stop en route, making this location a hive of activity especially during the summer season.

Andrew Kennedy

DEVON GENERAL
'Named Buses'

Plate 270: The tradition of naming Devon General double deckers has existed since 1919 when three 'B' types were named: *Sir Francis Drake*, *Sir John Hawkins*, and *Sir Walter Raleigh*, names still carried by three convertible open-top Leyland PDR1 vehicles with Metro-Cammell bodywork. On 20th October 1981, one of the eleven convertible open-toppers, built by Eastern Coachworks for Western National in 1977, out of the 50 manufactured at the time, was seen near the harbour at Torquay. Although some of these vehicles operate in Cornwall, all eleven carry the red and white livery and No. 938 (VDV 138S) pictured here, advertises the Torbay Freedom Bus Ticket. All eleven of these vehicles are named after famous warships, this particular bus being named *Warspite* and carrying the Devon General fleetname.

Rex Kennedy

Plate 271: The fascination of seeing a double deck bus in two different modes, once with a roof and another time without, is intriguing. In this view, a Devon General Bristol VR, No. 938 *Warspite* (VDV 138S), picks up holidaymakers high above the River Dart at Kingswear on 26th July 1981. The comparison between this and the last picture is interesting, now showing the vehicle in its 'open-top' state. Whilst not in use, the roofs of these vehicles are stacked on chassis frames in the garages to which the vehicles are allocated.

Colin Caddy

Plate 272: In 1961 Devon General introduced its 'Sea Dog' class, naming nine Leyland Atlantean convertible open-top double deckers, with Metro-Cammell bodywork, after famous seafarers. Some of these vehicles are still running today in the Torbay area and some also in Cornwall. All vehicles carry the red and white livery, and on 20th October 1981, No. 928 *Sir Humphrey Gilbert*, (928 GTA), with its roof fitted, heads from Teignmouth with a Torquay service along the coast road, which at this point overlooks Labrador Bay. As the evening sun goes down, the upper part of the vehicle is highlighted and at this time of day the low sun creates a driving hazard.

Rex Kennedy

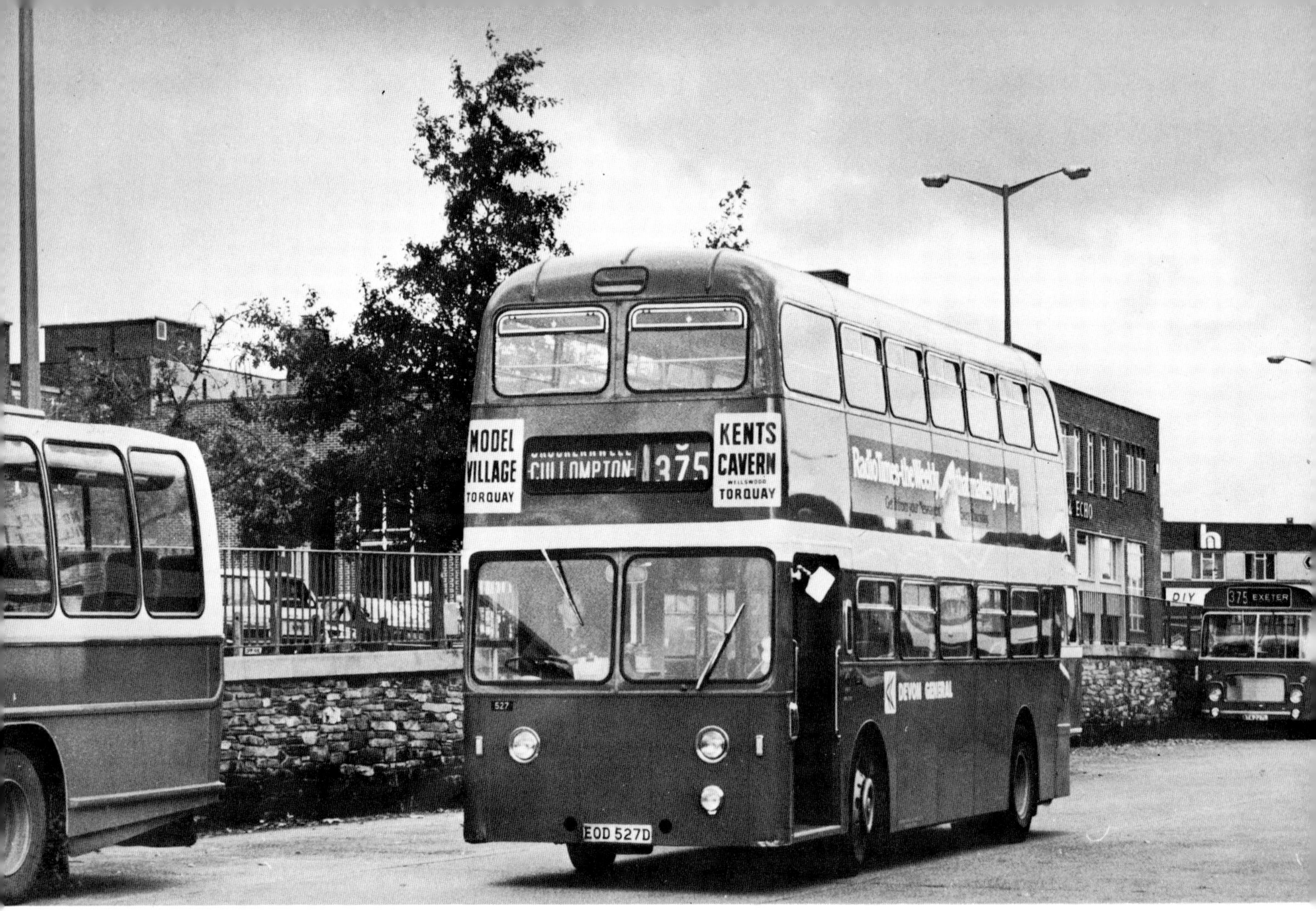

Plate 273: Exeter bus station is a hive of activity, the upper level dealing with bus service routes and the lower section handling express coach services. On 20th October 1981, Devon General, No. 527 (EOD 527D), a Leyland Atlantean with 75 seat Willowbrook body, leaves the upper section with a service for Cullompton. The original colour used by Devon General prior to joining the NBC organisation was cherry red, and many of the vehicles which carry the Devon General fleetname today run in the poppy red livery. However, from November 1979, as these vehicles entered workshops they were repainted in the NBC corporate leaf green livery as used on Western National buses. No. 527 is pictured here wearing the green livery having received its change of colour when outshopped from the works in August 1981.

Rex Kennedy

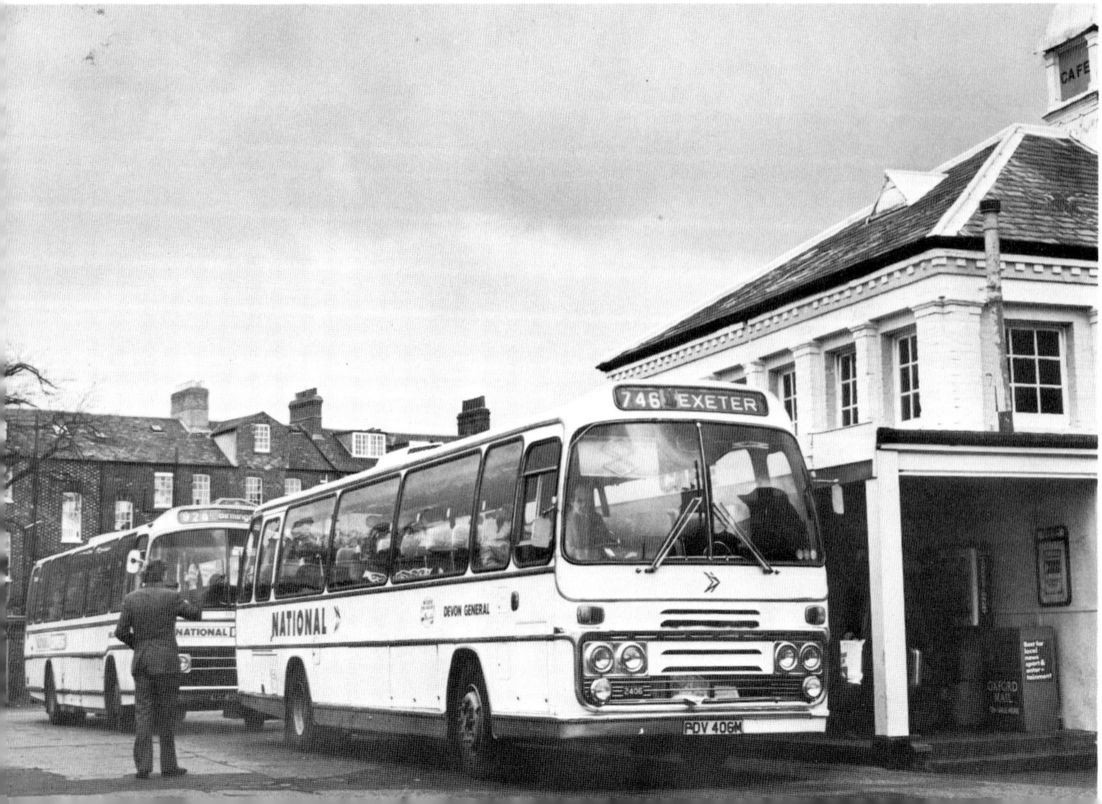

Plate 274: On 4th January 1981, a Devon General Bristol RELH coach, No. 2406 (PDV 406M), with Plaxton bodywork, pauses at the bus station at Gloucester Green, Oxford with a winter service before continuing its journey to Exeter. This vehicle carries an oval sticker behind the fleetname, celebrating 100 years of Royal Blue express coach services 1880-1980, Royal Blue and Devon General, being, of course, subsidiary companies of the Western National organisation. By July 1981, No. 2406 carried a Western National fleetname. Behind this vehicle is a Midland Red Plaxton bodied Leyland Leopard, No. 616 (NOE 616R), with a Birmingham service for connection to Liverpool.

Rex Kennedy

Trainee and Advertising Buses

Plate 275: The correct description of this scene is 'Driver Under Instruction', as ex-Hants & Dorset 1962 Bristol FS, with ECW bodywork, climbs away from Taunton on 20th October 1981 with a driver 'learning the ropes'. This particular vehicle is now in the Western National fleet and carries the number TV7 (4384 LJ), and when with Hants & Dorset was numbered 1126. Prior to 1972 when the amalgamation between Hants & Dorset and Wilts & Dorset took place, this vehicle was numbered 1461. It is one of four of this type of bus acquired from Hants & Dorset by Western National which still remain as trainee vehicles. It is interesting to note that the fleet number, although on a 'trainee' bus, is on the same style plate as the service buses.
Andrew Kennedy

Plate 276: All-over advertising buses create a small problem when the company fleetname needs to be shown somewhere on the vehicle. On Bristol VR No. 1082 (GTA 52N) the operator's name, 'Western National' appears across the radiator grille. This particular 'advertiser', pictured in Taunton town centre on a local service on 20th October 1981, is in a black livery and certainly serves its purpose as an advertiser as it passes through the town.
Andrew Kennedy

Bristol LH Designs

Plate 277: The rather unusual design of a Bristol LH with long chassis and 37 seat Marshall body, is pictured at Totnes on 20th October 1981. This Western National vehicle, No. 1316 (BDV 316L), prepares to pull empty into the small area reserved for parking buses in the square near the river at Totnes. This location once had its own Western National garage which closed on 30th May 1981 and ten years ago had an allocation of over twenty vehicles, which included double deckers and coaches. Western National purchased ten of this type of vehicle in 1973, adding yet another coach builder to the Bristol LH complement in their fleet already rich in ECW and Duple bodied versions. Later they acquired Bristol LHs with Plaxton bodies.
Rex Kennedy

Plate 279: Greenslades, whose garage is situated in Exeter south of the river, was formed in 1912 at Bradninch, near Exeter and once carried a livery of buff and green and also advertised their 'Silent Guide' coaches feature on their vehicles. The unique 'Silent Guide' feature was introduced in the 1930s and provided, to all passengers, detailed booklets with numbered paragraphs. At the point where the coach passed a place of interest detailed in the booklet, the driver would pull a lever in his cab which rang a bell and a number would appear above the clock at the front of the coach which would indicate the particular paragraph referring to the place of interest being passed at that time. After the introduction of public address systems, the driver would just speak the paragraph number into his microphone. Needless to say, this scheme has now been abandoned. In 1971 Greenslades took over the Grey Cars Coach Company. Grey Cars were to Devon General what Royal Blue was to Western National, representing their respective main coaching fleets. Greenslades eventually became National Travel (South West) together with Wessex, Black & White Motorways and Shamrock & Rambler, the latter now reverting to Hants & Dorset. On 20th October 1981, Bristol LH coach No. 326 (JFJ 506N) with the narrower 7ft. 6in. wide Plaxton body, stands parked at Exeter coach station. However, although this vehicle appears to carry a National Travel (South West) fleet number, in May 1981 all Exeter based 'South West' coaches, the majority carrying the fleetname 'Greenslades', were transferred to Western National. These vehicles were not given the standard Western National fleet number on a metal plate, as the numbers carried by these coaches did not clash with others in their fleet.
Rex Kennedy

Plate 280: In the special blue and white 'Sealink' livery, Leyland National No. 2823 (MOD 823P) of the Western National fleet, stands at Weymouth together with its ex-B.E.A. trailer No. T1 in May 1981. This unusual combination is used between Weymouth Town station situated near the Western National garage, and Weymouth Quay station. This vehicle is used for conveying passengers and their luggage to the Channel Island ferry on the quay at Weymouth. No. 2823 was painted in this smart livery in September 1980.

Colin Caddy

Plate 278: One of the Devon General Marshall bodied short chassis Bristol LHs, No. 90 (VOD 90K), sporting the poppy red livery, stands at the exit to the 'sawtooth' design bus station at Exeter on 20th October 1981. Six of these unusual vehicles with rear window design similar to the front windscreen, were delivered to Devon General in 1972 and are fitted with 33 seats. These unique vehicles were numbered 88–93 but now the batch is slowly dwindling in numbers as some have been withdrawn. These vehicles, when new, carried the original Devon General livery of cherry red with white above the waist.

Rex Kennedy

Plate 281: The 'Southern Coastlink' express X35 service operated by Western National covers the route from Southwell to Bournemouth via Portland, Weymouth and Poole. Carrying the special X35 livery, No. 1087 (LOD 727F), a 1975 Bristol VR, with ECW bodywork, stands at Weymouth in July 1981. Many NBC vehicles now appear in special liveries relating to express service routes, but some differ from this vehicle in being fitted with coach type seating. Weymouth was originally a Southern National garage.

Brian Jackson

Plate 282: It was a sad day when Royal Blue lost their fine blue and cream livery and fell in line with all other NBC express coaches painted in white. On 4th April 1981, a Royal Blue Leyland Leopard, No. 2442 (SFJ 142R), fitted with Plaxton coachwork, stood in one of the coach lanes which make up the lower part of Exeter bus station, which, on summer Saturdays, is an extremely active location. 'Royal Blue' was founded by Thomas Elliott in 1880 at the age of 22, and at his home in Bournemouth was a glass covered yard which housed the stables and coach houses. During their 101 years of operation, Royal Blue built an excellent reputation, and ten years ago operated from two main garages, Bournemouth and London, with outstations at Exeter, Portsmouth, Salisbury and Southampton. They now seem to have lost most of their personal identity.

Andrew Kennedy

WEST RIDING YORKSHIRE

Plate 283: Certain coaches and dual purpose saloons in the West Riding fleet carry both West Riding and Yorkshire fleetnames above the windows, and on 28th August 1981 a 1971 Leyland Leopard PSU3, No. 329 (AHL 729K) of the West Riding fleet, fitted with Plaxton bodywork, awaits departure from Saville Street bus station, Wakefield, with a service for Middleton. The 247ft. spire of the 15th Century parish church, which was given Cathedral status in 1888, overlooks this bus station. The reason for the dual fleetnames on certain West Riding vehicles is derived from the formation by NBC of the 'West Riding' group, originally incorporating West Riding, Yorkshire Woollen District and Hebble vehicles, with Wakefield becoming the head office. However, Hebble eventually became National Travel (North East) and is now National Travel (East).

Rex Kennedy

Plate 284: A West Riding Leyland National Mk. 1, No. 46 (CWX 664T), passes beneath one of the many brick arches which carry the railway above the highways of Leeds. On 2nd August 1981, this vehicle prepares to turn into the busy Central bus station. West Riding Automobile Co. Ltd. have had Leylands in the fleet since 1926 and the tradition continues today. West Riding does not operate a garage in Leeds itself, although it is geographically in the West Riding of Yorkshire. However, regular services run into this location from other parts of the West Riding/Yorkshire network, such as Wakefield and Dewsbury.

Rex Kennedy

Plate 285: Dewsbury has been the headquarters of the Yorkshire Woollen District Transport Co. Ltd. since its formation. It is appropriately named as the town of Dewsbury is at the centre of the heavy woollen industry in the West Riding of Yorkshire. The architecture in this part of Britain always makes a fine photographic background, especially the many stone viaducts and bridges which always seem to enhance the industrial north. On 15th November 1981, a 'Yorkshire' Bristol VR, No. 778 (RYG 387R), passes beneath one of the photogenic railway arches in Dewsbury on a service to Cleckheaton. The dual West Yorkshire PTE/NBC crest appears below the windscreen. This combined crest can be seen on NBC vehicles working within the PTE area.

Andrew Kennedy

Plate 286: Passing over the railway bridge which traverses the busy main railway lines from Sheffield to Leeds at Normanton, in West Yorkshire, a 1970 West Riding Bristol RELL, No. 305 (UHL 938J), with ECW bodywork, enters the town of Normanton having just passed through Altofts with a local service on 19th September 1981. In 1950 the West Riding fleet was nearly doubled in size when they took over the major bus operator in the Wakefield area, J. Bullock & Sons. Although their main garage was at Featherstone, one of their smaller garages was situated in Normanton.

Rex Kennedy

Plate 287: A line up of West Riding double deckers stand proudly in the sunshine on 2nd August 1981 in the yard adjacent to Featherstone garage. These six vehicles comprise five Daimlers and one Leyland Atlantean. The Roe bodied 1966 Atlantean stands out from the other vehicles in the line in having white livery and being a driver trainer vehicle, No. A 22 (EHL 700D). Its fleet number, prior to becoming a 'trainee' vehicle, was 566. The Daimler Fleetlines in the line up show two differing designs. No. 663 (PHL 228G), withdrawn in May 1981, No. 637 (MHL 302F) and No. 636 (MHL 301F) all carry Roe bodywork, whereas No. 672 (WHL 274J) and No. 675 (WHL 277J) are fitted with Alexander bodies. The Roe Coach Works, of course, is a Yorkshire Company situated in Leeds. As many collieries are located in this area, vehicles allocated to Featherstone garage work on services to and from the pits.

Rex Kennedy

Plate 288: A Bristol VR, No. 461 (RUA 461W), licenced in March 1981 and carrying the 'Yorkshire' fleetname, pulls into Huddersfield bus station on 28th August 1981. This vehicle is operating a Huddersfield to Leeds service, and the large bus station at Huddersfield sees a variety of Yorkshire company operators including West Yorkshire PTE and South Yorkshire PTE vehicles. Off duty vehicles are parked against the wall away from the pick up points, giving ample room for buses to reverse away from this 'sawtooth' design location before departure.

Rex Kennedy

Plate 289: The open area making up Heath Common, to the east of Wakefield, is the scene for one of the last Bristol VRs to enter the West Riding fleet. No. 472 (VUA 472X) climbs out of Wakefield with a Sunday service to Castleford on 15th November 1981. The town of Wakefield in the background is overpowered by the ever active power station situated on the edge of the Common. This vehicle carries the joint West Yorkshire PTE/NBC crest together with the name 'Metrobus' in large letters taking priority over the West Riding fleetname on the side of the vehicle, and was diverted to West Riding from a York/West Yorkshire order.
Rex Kennedy

Plate 290: The joint West Yorkshire PTE and NBC logos together with the West Riding and Metrobus wording and slogan as it appears on the vehicle pictured above.
Rex Kennedy

Plate 291: Two 13ft. 8in. West Riding Bristol VRT double deckers stand in the yard at Belle Isle depot, Wakefield on 28th August 1981. The two vehicles on view, Nos. 758 (NWR 507P) and 752 (MUA 874P) carry varying fleetnames. No. 758 carries the large fleet number and 'Metrobus'/NBC joint fleetnames and crests, whereas No. 752 is seen in normal NBC livery. Belle Isle is the headquarters for the West Riding fleet and covers a vast area with spacious covered accommodation, sizeable works and paintshops and parking beside the River Calder. West Riding, prior to 1967, were one of the largest independents in England when they were placed under the ownership of The Transport Holding Company. In 1969, of course, ownership passed to the National Bus Company together with others in the THC and BEC groups. West Riding's original livery was green and certain vehicles have been painted in the old style livery. However, when the NBC corporate livery was introduced, poppy red was chosen for West Riding vehicles which brought them into line with the red livery once carried by Yorkshire Woollen buses incorporated into the West Riding group.
Rex Kennedy

Alexanders

Plate 292: The most easterly garage within the West Riding network is at Selby. This garage has a long standing reputation for providing excellent vehicle maintenance, and on Friday, 28th August 1981, two Alexander bodied vehicles and one with Marshall bodywork stood in the back of this comparatively small garage. The two West Riding/Yorkshire Alexander 'T' type vehicles, Nos. 3 (PWW 708R) and 4 (PWW 709R) carry differing liveries, No. 3 (dual-purpose) and No. 4 (express coach). These two vehicles comprise half the 'T' type complement in the West Riding fleet. No. 326 (AHL 726K), a Plaxton bodied Leyland Leopard, stands against the wall. Although Selby is now geographically situated in North Yorkshire, it was originally in the West Riding, hence the reason for this fleet operating in this area. Bus services in Selby sometimes suffer in their timetable schedules as the swing bridge over the River Ouse creates long traffic delays at certain times.

Rex Kennedy

Plate 293: A dual purpose Leyland Leopard, No. 383 (HWY 723N) of the West Riding fleet fitted with 49 seat Alexander 'Y' type bodywork and carrying the combined West Riding/Yorkshire fleetnames, leaves the station approach at Wakefield Westgate station on 15th November 1981 whilst on hire for the day to British Rail. The 'Leyland Leopard' plate affixed above the radiator adds to the character of this vehicle. In August 1981, this vehicle was seen without the 'Leopard' plate carrying a second NBC logo in this position. Eleven of this design of vehicle were purchased by West Riding in 1975 and all remained in service at the end of 1981.

Rex Kennedy

WEST YORKSHIRE

Plate 294: A typical rural scene in the Yorkshire Dales. With the rolling hills in the background, a West Yorkshire 52 seat Leyland National Mk. 2, No. 1511 (PNW 604W), passes through Low Laithes near Pateley Bridge, and proceeds towards Harrogate with an afternoon service from Pateley Bridge on 14th November 1981. This vehicle is on a return service which, at this time of year, is less patronised than it is in the summer.

Rex Kennedy

Plate 295: Awaiting departure for Skipton from the bus station at Grassington on 14th November 1981, is No. 1006 (DNW 844T), one of the earlier 10.3 metre Series 'B' Leyland Nationals in the West Yorkshire fleet. This particular bus station, which is also used as a sub garage for Skipton allocated buses, was built in 1958.

Andrew Kennedy

Plate 296: A Skipton based West Yorkshire 52 seat 11.3 metre Leyland National Mk. 1, No. 1482 (TYG 741R), nears the end of its country service from Grassington as it approaches the outskirts of Skipton on 14th November 1981. Ribble also operate services into Skipton from Burnley, and until 1976 Skipton itself was once the location of a Ribble garage. Upon closure of this garage, Ribble vehicles were kept at the West Yorkshire garage for a while.

Andrew Kennedy

Plate 297: Vicar Lane bus station in Leeds is used solely by the West Yorkshire Road Car Co. Ltd. for services from Leeds to other areas in the West Yorkshire network. This comparatively small bus station creates quite difficult manoeuvring problems, being of the 'sawtooth' design, necessitating careful reversing from the pick up points into a small area before departure. On 16th September 1981, a West Yorkshire Bristol VR, No. 1755 (PWY 41W), moves on to this bus station in preparation to pick up passengers for Otley. It is noticeable that this particular vehicle carries the joint West Yorkshire PTE/NBC crest and 'Metrobus' insignia displayed on buses operating within the PTE area.

Rex Kennedy

Plate 298: Prior to receiving the fleet number 2608 soon after being delivered new to the West Yorkshire fleet, a Leyland PSU3 coach, Regn. No. UWY 86X, with Duple Dominant 49 seat bodywork, stands outside Harrogate garage on 28th August 1981 still sporting its 'Duple Coachworks' sticker in the window. This vehicle carries the red and white local coach livery. The West Yorkshire garage at Harrogate was opened in 1927 and extended in 1934, and a West Yorkshire works is also situated at Harrogate.

Rex Kennedy

Plate 299: A reflected image of the smallest variety of Leyland National in the guise of West Yorkshire's No. 1002 (DNW 840T), a 44 seat 10.3 metre 'Baby National', as it stands at Harrogate bus station on Easter Monday 1981 before departing for Boroughbridge. The Series 'B' Leyland National, its official title, is not fitted with the conventional 'pod' and was the new design 'National' announced by Leyland in 1978 as the new 'economy' version. The front panel incorporates three sets of vents, clearly visible in this view, fitted in connection with the substitute heating and ventilation system which replaced the 'pod' heating system fitted to earlier models.

Andrew Kennedy

Harrogate

YORK City Buses

Plate 301: A fleet of over 100 Bristol RELL6G ECW bodied service buses was once owned by The West Yorkshire Road Car Co., the majority being fitted with 53 seats. No. 3234 (PYG 652E), one of the few 52 seat variety built in 1967, stands at York on Easter Saturday 1981 bearing, in gold lettering, the 'York-West Yorkshire' logo, a style no longer used since the introduction of the name 'York' together with the city crest on the side of all York based service buses in the West Yorkshire fleet. During one of the major renumbering schemes within the company in October 1971, this particular vehicle was renumbered from SRG34. Soon after this picture was taken, No. 3234 was withdrawn from service and sold to a dealer in Lincoln.

Andrew Kennedy

Plate 300: One of the oldest double decker buses remaining in the West Yorkshire fleet, No. 3950 (DWU 835H), a 1970 Bristol VRT, passes within the city walls at York with a local service on 16th September 1981. This vehicle is of the lowbridge short wheelbase variety of VR with a transverse engine and bears the 'York' fleetname now used, since April 1981, on locally allocated West Yorkshire buses after the old 'York-West Yorkshire' fleetname was discontinued. No. 3950 is fitted with a fare box for collecting exact fares whilst on service. Only York and Keighley garages operate fare box vehicles. York Minster, Lendal Bridge and the wall of this fine old city, make an ideal setting for this picture.

Rex Kennedy

Plate 302: An 11.3 metre Leyland National Mk. 1, No. 3430 (NWT 712M), bearing the 'York-West Yorkshire' fleetname, passes a Bristol VR and climbs away with a local service from the Station Hotel, York, on a sunny Easter Saturday in 1981. Of the York allocated West Yorkshire fleet, service buses commence with a '3' in their four digit fleet numbers, whereas dual purpose vehicles and coaches are in the 1000 or 2000 series.

Andrew Kennedy

Plate 303: Awaiting its next journey on the 'City Tour' of York, a West Yorkshire 1976 Leyland PSU3 Plaxton 49 seat coach, No. 2329 (RYG 537R), stands in the sunshine outside York railway station on 16th September 1981. This service is, of course, very popular at Easter when crowds flock to York and also in the height of the summer. Owing to its historical background, York is one of the more popular inland holiday resorts in Britain.

Rex Kennedy

Plate 304: The West Yorkshire garage at Malton is situated near the railway station and is the furthest east of all West Yorkshire garages verging on United and East Yorkshire territory. This view, on Easter Monday 1981, shows two 1969 British ECW bodied REs, Nos. 1297 (BYG 543H) and 1298 (BYG 855H) both in the West Yorkshire fleet, with the more common 53 seating arrangement. Both these vehicles were withdrawn from service by West Yorkshire in May 1981 and by the end of the year, No. 1297 was being operated by City Bus of Belfast, and No. 1298 had been sold to a dealer in Lincoln. These two vehicles prior to October 1971 carried the fleet numbers YSRG97 and YSRG98. In October 1971 they were renumbered 3297 and 3298 as part of the 'York-West Yorkshire' fleet and on transfer to the main West Yorkshire fleet were again renumbered 1297 and 1298. The vehicle to the right of the picture is a 10.3 metre Series 'B' National, No. 1003 (DNW 841T).
Andrew Kennedy

West Yorkshire Garages

Plate 305: A West Yorkshire Plaxton bodied 49 seat RELH coach, No. 2544 (RWY 636M), previously numbered 2322 until early 1981, passes through the wash in York's West Yorkshire garage on Easter Monday 1981. This garage has an allocation of approximately 100 vehicles, being the largest allocation of any garage in the West Yorkshire network, followed by Bradford, Keighley and Leeds.
Andrew Kennedy

Plate 306: Two withdrawn West Yorkshire ECW bodied Bristol RELH 47 seater coaches, Nos. 2514 (YYG 217G) and 2515 (YWY 514G), lie at the rear of Harrogate West Yorkshire garage on 28th August 1981. This particular year saw the phasing out of this model from the West Yorkshire fleet, a design which will be sadly missed by the modern bus enthusiast.
Rex Kennedy

YORKSHIRE TRACTION

Plate 307: Carrying the smart poppy red with broad white band dual purpose livery befitting this style of single deck bus, one of Yorkshire Traction's Leyland Leopards, No. 144 (LHL 244P), with Alexander 'T' type body, leaves its home garage of Doncaster to return to duty. This 1976 model shows the improved radiator grille introduced in that year by Alexander Coachbuilders of Scotland. The 'T' type was first introduced in 1974 and was designed to be suitable as a service coach, touring coach or even a long distance express coach. This vehicle was renumbered from No. 244 in 1980. Doncaster operates two large bus stations, one mainly Yorkshire Traction and the other predominantly South Yorkshire PTE.

Rex Kennedy

Plate 308: A Yorkshire Traction Daimler Fleetline, No. 753 (XHE 753J), with Park Royal bodywork, passes the Queens Hotel in Barnsley before stopping to pick up more passengers on its Sunday service. Pictured on 15th November 1981, No. 753 was one of five 1971 'Fleetlines', now in the Yorkshire Traction fleet, originally ordered by Sheffield Joint Omnibus Committee. These 76 seat single doored vehicles even included 'Sheffield's' traditional front bumper bar as seen in this view.

Rex Kennedy

Plate 309: Before turning into the bus station at Barnsley on 15th November 1981, No. 663 (RHE 663G) of the Yorkshire Traction fleet, a 1969 Daimler Fleetline with Northern Counties bodywork, negotiates the level crossing near the station. The panoramic side windows were a feature introduced in 1967 and this vehicle is fitted with a fully glazed two section door. On the earlier Northern Counties bodied double deckers fitted to Leyland chassis ordered by Yorkshire Traction in 1967, curved windscreens were fitted, whereas No. 663, pictured here, carries the split windscreen.

Andrew Kennedy

Plate 311: On a gloomy winter's day, 28th February 1981, a Yorkshire Traction Bristol VR, No. 918 (EDT 918V), with ECW bodywork, pulls up at a bus stop in the small town of Sprotbrough near Doncaster. This vehicle is one of the 16ft. 2in. wheelbase Bristol VRs fitted with a Leyland engine and carries the 13ft. 8in. standard lowbridge body.

Adrian Foster

Plate 312: On 28th August 1981, No. 58 (DAK 258V), a Plaxton bodied Leyland Leopard coach stood in the yard at Huddersfield garage. It is apparent from the small window stickers that in this day and age the vast majority of seating accommodation on NBC coaches is specifically for use by non-smoking travellers. Huddersfield Yorkshire Traction garage has an allocation of approximately 30 vehicles, these chiefly being Leyland Nationals and Bristol VRs. About 40% of the Yorkshire Traction fleet is allocated to Barnsley garage with the remaining vehicles, in addition to those at the Huddersfield garage, being based at Doncaster, Rawmarsh, Shafton and Wombwell garages.

Rex Kennedy

Plate 310: In April 1980, Yorkshire Traction painted one of their vehicles in the original pre-war livery, and placed this vehicle on display at an Open Day at Barnsley garage on 20th April 1980. The vehicle chosen was No. 864 (TDT 864S), a 1978 Bristol VRT with ECW bodywork. The old style numbering and lettering certainly enhances the vehicle as it climbs the hill into Barnsley on 15th November 1981 on a Cudworth service. The present Yorkshire Traction name was adopted in 1928 and prior to this, from 1902, was the Barnsley District Electric Traction Company.

Andrew Kennedy

Plate 313: The large NBC bus station at Barnsley lies adjacent to the railway station. This location is a hive of activity, even on a Sunday afternoon, with steady movement of vehicles both in and out on service. The constant sound of horns as buses reverse to take out their services is quite deafening at times, but this idea, of course, cuts down the risk of accidents. On 15th November 1981, Yorkshire Traction No. 375 (CHE 375K), a 1972 Leyland Leopard with a 53 seat Marshall body, stands beside the exit of Barnsley bus station together with a Leyland National in the all-red livery.

Andrew Kennedy

NATIONAL TRAVEL EAST

Plate 314: National Travel, in addition to operating fast efficient express services throughout Britain, also hire out their vehicles for private charter. On 14th November 1981, a great deal of activity was going on in the Yorkshire town of Skipton in Airedale incorporating a carnival type atmosphere including a parade through the town. For this occasion the Hawley Band had been invited to take part, and they arrived in one of the new National Travel (East) coaches. The vehicle used, (NHL 259X), a Plaxton bodied Leyland PSU5, new in September 1981, was to be found in a very congested car park in Skipton near to the bus station from which West Yorkshire, Ribble and the local independent Pennine Motor Services operate. This vehicle, in addition to LHE 253W, also in the National Travel (East) fleet, is fitted with a television for the benefit of travellers.

Andrew Kennedy

Plate 315: National Travel was formed in 1973/74, being split into five areas, Midlands, North East, South West, North West and South East. Since the initial formation, changes have been made with North West and Midlands becoming West, South East being renamed London, North East changing to East, and South West keeping its original name. National Travel (East) incorporated Sheffield United Tours and Hebble of Liversedge. Ex-National Travel (South East) Leyland Leopard ULW 490M with 51 seat Plaxton bodywork arrives at Sheffield with a London service on 2nd August 1981. This vehicle was acquired from National Travel (London) in May 1980.

Geoff Mills

Plate 316: The National Travel (East) garage at Frost Hill, Liversedge, pictured here, is a former Yorkshire Woollen Company depot. On 28th August 1981, three National Travel (East) coaches stood against the wall of the garage. NHL 260X, a Leyland PSU5 with Plaxton coachwork was delivered in August 1981, but was originally scheduled to carry the number LHE 260W had it been delivered prior to August. At the rear of the garage a glimpse can be seen of JKU 451P which had been recently painted in special red and blue livery on a white background to operate on the Leeds—Manchester—Liverpool service, a livery also carried by certain West Yorkshire NBC coaches. A further vehicle, JKU 449P was also painted in a similar livery. After the formation of British Coachways by a group of independent operators, resulting from the new Transport Act of October 1980 making it unnecessary to obtain a service licence for express routes over 30 miles, a price cutting war was commenced involving British Coachways charging half National Travel fares over certain routes. As a result of this move, National Travel have now set out to improve their image with each operator being given almost a 'free hand' to improve their vehicles. Improvements made to National Travel (East) coaches, instigated by the General Manager, are to include headrest covers, curtains and wheel trims.

Rex Kennedy

NATIONAL TRAVEL LONDON

Plate 317: Carrying the special 'London Transport Coach Tours' livery of white with red skirt and roof, a Bedford YMT, Regn. No. BGY 599T, fitted with Duple bodywork, an attractive looking National Travel (London) coach, stands in the building used for washing vehicles near Victoria coach station, London on 10th October 1981. Painting of the vehicle in this special livery took place in April 1981 and a similar livery was applied to BGY 597T. On 1st January 1979 when National Travel (London) was formed, eighty-six vehicles were taken over from National Travel (South East) followed by large withdrawals after new vehicles were purchased by National Travel (London) early in 1979.
Andrew Kennedy

Plate 318: The large coach and car park at Windsor overlooked by the Castle is usually fairly bare during winter months. However, Windsor always seems to carry an attraction for a certain amount of visitors all year round. On 13th December 1981, the snow covered coach park was the resting place for three independent operators' coaches and a National Travel (London) 1979 AEC Reliance, Regn. No. BGY 581T, with a Plaxton body, as it stood parked beneath the snow clad trees. National Travel (London) was the new name used from 1st January 1979 on vehicles previously in the National Travel (South East) fleet which was originally formed in 1974. National Travel (South East) incorporated Tillings, Timpsons and Samuelsons with the Eastern National coaching fleet and Mascot coaches being added later. On the change of name to National Travel (London), the Eastern National coaches returned to their parent company.
Rex Kennedy

NATIONAL TRAVEL   SOUTH WEST

Cheltenham Coach Station.

Plate 320: The many bays under cover of St. Margaret's Road coach station, Cheltenham, are a hive of activity around 11a.m. and 3p.m. especially on summer Saturdays, and have been so since Associated Motorways was formed in 1934. This organisation was created by the amalgamation of the coach fleets of Black & White Motorways, Bristol Tramways, Red & White, Royal Blue, Midland Red and United Counties to eliminate duplication of routes by these companies and others joining Associated Motorways later. The onslaught of vehicles arriving at Cheltenham resulted in a vast variety of liveries in one place, making it far easier for passengers to find their particular coach than today with confusion often arising as all vehicles are in the NBC corporate white livery. On 28th November 1981, No. 101 (PDD 101M), a National Travel (South West) Duple bodied Leyland Leopard, stands in Bay 1 during a complete lull of arrivals and departures. The coach station at Cheltenham has changed very little since the 1950s, except that coaches now also load in the uncovered area to the rear of the covered bays, an area once allocated to bus services for Bristol Tramways and Red & White to places such as Newport, Monmouth and Bristol.

Andrew Kennedy

Plate 319: St. Margaret's Road National Travel (South West) garage and coach station at Cheltenham was acquired by Black & White Motorways in June 1931, and at that time was regarded as the most up to date coach station of its kind outside London. This view, of the interior of the maintenance garage, shows the old 'Black & White Motorways' crest proudly hanging from the wall as National Travel (South West) Leyland Leopard, No. 223 (YDF323K), with Plaxton coachwork, stands in the garage on 24th August 1981.
Rex Kennedy

Plate 321: The building at St. Margaret's Road, Cheltenham, which, on 24th August 1981 housed National Travel (South West) Leyland Leopard No. 190 (AFH 190T), with Duple bodywork, portraying Cheltenham to Paris P & O Ferries service, was once used by Yelloway for loading passengers on their northbound coaches. Yelloway vehicles are still to be found at this location, but no longer have their own under-cover loading area. The livery of No. 190 is white with a pale blue skirt, and the rectangular England – Paris panel near the door, indicates that the service operates 'Direct From Cheltenham, Bristol, Bath, Salisbury and Southampton', National Travel's link with the continent. The flag seen beside the P & O Ferries name is in red, blue, yellow and white. Although 'South West' was the largest of the five original areas formed at the birth of National Travel in 1973, this is no longer the case since the loss of some of their fleet as detailed in **Plate 323**.
Rex Kennedy

Plate 322: On 24th August 1981, a Wessex 1973 Duple bodied Leyland Leopard, No. 245 (FDF 345L), of the National Travel (South West) fleet, is raised high with the help of hydraulic jacks whilst awaiting attention in the maintenance shops at Cheltenham. The Wessex division of the 'South West' fleet is based at Kingswood, Bristol, and in mid-1981 consisted of approximately forty-five vehicles representing about 40% of the National Travel (South West) fleet after the loss of Shamrock & Rambler, Greenslades and South Wales vehicles.
Rex Kennedy

Plate 323: National Travel (South West) now only incorporate Black & White Motorways and Wessex vehicles, having lost, during 1981, the Shamrock & Rambler fleet to Hants & Dorset, the Greenslades vehicles to Western National and the South Wales coach fleet to South Wales Transport which resulted in the loss of garaging facilities at Bournemouth, Exeter and Swansea. A 'Wessex' Plaxton bodied Leyland Leopard, No. 214 (XDG 214S), manoeuvres round the restrictive bus station at Drummer Street, Cambridge, in April 1981, portraying a route sticker on its side, not really indicative of the location at which it is pictured.
Kevin Lane

NATIONAL TRAVEL WEST

Plate 324: Passengers depart after collecting their luggage soon after the arrival of 1974 Duple bodied Leyland Leopard, No. N123 (TTF 223M), of the National Travel (West) fleet at Victoria coach station, London, in January 1981. It is surprising to see Victoria devoid of vehicles as under normal conditions the scene is one of constant arrivals and departures. This particular vehicle was ordered by the North Western Road Car Co. and was acquired from National Travel (North West) in April 1977. On 2nd November 1980 over 160 vehicles in the National Travel (West) fleet were renumbered, and prior to this date No. N123 carried the fleet number N127.

Kevin Lane

Plate 325: Victoria coach station, London is the centre for National Travel Express operations from the capital and receives coaches from all over Britain. A Leyland Leopard National Travel (West) No. 135 (TTF 235M), with Duple coachwork, was originally ordered by Standerwick, and was another vehicle acquired in April 1977 by National Travel (West) from (North West) having carried the fleet number N139 until November 1980. It awaits departure with an express service for Southport on 10th October 1981.

Andrew Kennedy

Plate 326: National Travel (West) operate from garages in Lancashire and was formed in 1977 incorporating National Travel (North West) and (Midlands), two of the original five companies which formed National Travel in 1973. The 'Midlands' section comprised the companies of Don Everall and Worthingtons and 'North West' vehicles were those of Standerwick and the North Western Road Car Co. The Ribble garage at Burnley is used for housing National Travel (West) vehicles, and on 14th November 1981, Leyland Leopard No. N251, (ex-1251), Regn. No. HNE 251V with Duple bodywork, sits just inside the garage entrance. National Travel (West) no longer operate from any garages in the Midlands.

Andrew Kennedy